A Deer Watcher's Field Guide

A Deer Watcher's Field Guide

Whitetails of the Midwest

by John H. Williams

Momentum Books, Ltd.
Troy, Michigan

Manufactured in the United States of America

Cover Design by Tim Bodendistel
Photographs by John H. Williams
Illustrations by Andrea Shields

ISBN: 1-879094-51-7

Williams, John H., 1946–
    A deer watcher's field guide : whitetails of the Midwest / by John H. Williams.
        p.   cm.
    Includes bibliographical references (p. 243)   and index.
    ISBN 1-879094-51-7 (pb : alk. paper)
    1. White-tailed deer—Middle West. 2. White-tailed deer—
—Behavior—Middle West.   I. Title.
QL737.U55W55   1996
599.73'57--dc20   95-43356
                                                        CIP

Dedication

This book is dedicated to the memory of three of the finest gentlemen, and sportsmen, I have ever known.

Gerald R. Breneman, M.D. 1925–1989
Harvey Joseph "Joe" Frankum 1945–1990
James "Bob" Kee 1927–1993

I miss them, their example, their influence, their insight and wisdom. They all made a difference. I shall never forget them.

Table of Contents

Cud chewing and self grooming behaviors take up a large percentage of any deer's day.

North America's white-tailed deer are magnificent creatures, their care and management demand no less than the best man can do. The author's concern, and he backs it up with valid, logical argument, is that, in many places, this is not the case. Far too often greed, self-centered motivation and, short-sighted monetary gain, dictate management decisions. Our wildlife management decisions must be based upon the good of the animals involved, not some ill perceived social values, however well intentioned.

Preface

In 1990, while putting together *The Deer Hunter's Field Guide: Pursuing Michigan's Whitetail,* Momentum Books' owner and president, Bill Haney, and one of my editors, Ed McGlinn, suggested I do another book of anecdotal stories of whitetails. Their feeling was that I'd had enough interesting encounters with deer to justify a sister publication to the *Field Guide.* To be honest, the whole idea turned me off—there are simply too many books in the marketplace already that have been written precisely in that manner. Nonetheless, the idea of a sister publication stuck in my mind and, over the next couple of months, I began to evolve the ideas behind this book, *Deer Watcher's Field Guide.*

I've been blessed throughout my life. I love the outdoors. I am fascinated by animals, and their behaviors. I've had the opportunity to travel, photograph, and hunt widely, from the arctic to Africa, and over much of North America. I've successfully hunted seventeen of North America's big game animals, but no animal, anywhere in the world, has ever had the hold on me that whitetails do. I've spent much of my life, personal and academic, trying to better understand them. As a writer I feel blessed too. This may sound arrogant. I do not intend it that way, but there is a simple honesty behind why I feel this way. Fortunately, I don't have to write for a living. I write because I enjoy doing so and, hopefully, I can give back something to a world that has given so much to me.

But, the fact that I don't have to write gives me an opportunity most writers don't have. I can take as long as I like—as long as is required—to complete the research and truly learn the facts behind what I write about. No one pays writers for the research they do. The publishing industry pays writers to write, and in order for full-time writers to earn a living they must produce written material, researched or not. That fact gives someone like me a tremendous advantage.

Rather than agree to do anecdotal experiences—I-think-so observation—Momentum and I decided I'd research the information for a new book for three years, then I'd write up my findings. This book is the culmination of those efforts. It's based on facts and observations from my study area in the southern portion of Michigan's "thumb" region. It's application and area of validity should be, however, much more extensive than that. Any region—Illinois, Indiana, Ohio, a lot of Pennsylvania, Kentucky, Tennessee, Missouri, Virginia, West Virginia, southern New York, southern Wisconsin, southern Minnesota, and elsewhere—having a similar climate (see the Introduction for a detailed climatological description of my study area), agriculturally based economy, and population parameters (human and deer) should witness behaviors among whitetails living there, as I studied here.

Deer Watcher's Field Guide is not a hunting book. It is a book written for anyone who has an interest in natural history and animal behaviors. A lot of the biological and behavioral information about deer found in this book will enable its readers to more fully understand animal observations and, hence, more fully enjoy their time afield. It certainly will benefit hunters as a companion to our earlier *Field Guide*, but it will also provide enjoyable insight to anyone interested in the natural world around them.

Acknowledgments

While I formulated, researched, then wrote *Deer Watcher's Field Guide* I couldn't have done so without the help and encouragement of many others.

First and foremost, my wife, Annette. She's always there, always understanding, always supportive. For that, I'll forever be thankful. I know I'm difficult, thanks. I couldn't and wouldn't have done it without you.

My editor and friend, Lawrence J. Gusman, Ph.D., deserves a hearty thank you! If this book is readable, in large measure it's through his efforts. Despite a very hectic professional life, Larry somehow found the time needed, and by so doing, has greatly strengthened the end result.

Andrea Shields, whose artwork graces these pages, has added immeasurably to the end product. Andrea is working towards her master's in social work: anyone looking through this book will realize that the social work world's gain is the art world's loss. Andrea, I wish I could change your mind—art is obviously *your* gift. Thank you.

Andrea's father, Don Shields, has been a friend for more than twenty years. I want to thank you, Don, for all the times, throughout the years, that you've listened attentively to my deer ramblings when, I know, you didn't have nearly as much interest as I did. I appreciate your patience and tolerance. Many others fall into that category too: John Chancey, Dick Kranz, Rich McClavish, Alice Wortman, and more. You folks have always been there, always supportive, which has done much to help keep me going. Thank you all.

I also want to thank all the people at Momentum Books Ltd., but especially Kyle Scott, their Marketing Director, and my editor there, Frank DePirro; their professionalism has made it all come together. If the total package you're now reading and looking at pleases you, it's because of their uncompromising ideals, and commitment to details.

I want to thank all the landowners, who, through their understanding, have made this study and these photographs possible. Obviously, I couldn't have done it without your support.

Lastly, a very special thank you to Leslie Kobayashi, Park Superintendent at Pinery/Ipperwash Provincial Parks in Grand Bend, Ontario. Without Les' trust, faith, and assistance, most of the photographs included here would not have been taken, especially those of the bigger, more mature bucks.

Introduction

This book is the result of three years of field observations and study, and of pouring through innumerable books, research papers, and magazines devoted to the white-tailed deer. Despite having spent years of my life, personal and academic, studying wildlife, it's been an eye opening three years for me. The real reason I wanted to do this work was because I felt (feel) that a high percentage of what's written about the whitetail, both in the popular press and in the scientific literature and management journals, is off base. It doesn't describe the behaviors and the life of the animal that I see day in and day out in my area.

Specific examples: Rutting behaviors: Sign-making behaviors, tending behaviors, intensity of behaviors, and so forth, do not coincide with what I've observed in southeastern Michigan for many years. Poaching: Prior to this work I felt it was a moderately severe threat to the whitetail in my area; now, three years later, I'm convinced that it's the biggest threat to our deer, next to habitat destruction. What's more, and I strongly believe this is something legitimate hunters had better wake up to, poaching and poachers are a real threat to hunting, since I don't believe most people really separate the two groups. Like it or not, hunters will lose more and more at the ballot box simply because the average citizen in this country will lump hunters and poachers together. Deer groupings: The formation of "bachelor groups" and the separation of bucks and does doesn't occur here as it apparently does in many areas. As I discuss throughout the body of the work, there are other variations, too.

Due to the terribly skewed condition of Michigan's deer herd, and the high nutritional plane under which they exist, gender separation, apparently so common elsewhere, is not nearly as evident here.

I believe these differences, and overall deer patterns and behaviors, can be understood based on three primary factors: (1) the prevailing weather patterns, (2) the management program of the state of Michigan, and (3) human demographics. Prevailing weather dictates, of course, growing seasons, the nutritional plane of the deer, and the nutritional stress levels they experience. The management program (see Chapter 8) dictates the parameters—deer densities, buck:doe ratios, and age-class structure—under which the deer live, and as we'll see this has tremendous ramifications for shaping their behaviors. Human demographics, including the economic and social stability of an area, income levels, occupations, and human density figures, have profound effects on the deer.

My study area was located in southern Lapeer County, Michigan. This is an agricultural/small industry-based area with a variety of small grain crops grown. These include mainly corn, wheat, alfalfa, barley, oats, clover, and soybeans. There are very few specialty crops. There are healthy dairy farming operations, hence cattle are common. Industry includes metalworking and sand and gravel mining operations. Soils range from a sandy loam to clay loams. The terrain ranges from level to gently rolling. Elevation is roughly 730 feet above sea level. Annual precipitation is between twenty-eight and thirty inches. Average annual snowfall is from forty to sixty inches. The human population of the county has more than doubled in the past twenty years and continues to grow rapidly, increasing roughly 6 percent to 7 percent annually. Farming has dwindled in direct proportion as this population growth has occurred. As I'll discuss in the text, I believe this change in demographics to be particularly important. Many of the "old-timers" witnessing such changes seem to lose their psychological ties to the land and its animals, and the new arrivals never had it. I believe this accounts, at least partially, for rampant poaching, trespassing, and a general disregard for the wildlife.

The specific area of my study is roughly fifty miles north of Detroit and forty-five miles west of Lake Huron. There is some lake effect as a result, but it's minimal and

Foreword

My first reaction to the idea of helping edit John's manuscript for publication was, "Oh, right. I'm a psychologist, not a hunter. I've never even seen a deer! I'm just the person he needs."

But I wasn't two paragraphs into the job before I had to know more about these intelligent, playful animals. And, of course, John taught me all I needed to know. By the time I was through, I'd learned more about the whitetail than I could have imagined possible.

I hope the readers of the book have the same experience I had. I found John's book like a walk in the woods with a personal guide—your favorite camp counselor or your favorite uncle. He makes each thicket come alive with his stories and his know-how, and I hope I haven't lost any of the fresh, down-to-earth flavor of his style as I rearranged some of his words for clarity or for a more standard usage.

John really has a passion about the deer—if that doesn't come through clearly, I *have* botched the job—and he is also a painstaking scientist. That combination makes him the best teacher one could hope for.

I am grateful to have been included on this adventure.

—Lawrence J. Gusman, Ph.D.

mainly involves autumn cloud cover. Winds are generally moderate at about 10 mph and westerly in direction, but there's a lot of variation both in velocity and direction. Approximately 40 percent of the land mass consists of agricultural lands. Ten percent of this is pasture land; the other 90 percent is crop fields or fallow fields, depending upon the year. Fifty percent of the land is covered by tree growth. Hardwoods predominate, but mast-bearing hardwoods (mostly oaks, with some beech and hickory) only comprise 10 percent of the total, and they tend to grow in select mixed stands along with maples and slippery elm. Planted pines cover less than 5 percent of the land, and they grow only in small, widely scattered plots. They range in size from three to fifteen acres. There are very few naturally occurring conifers. Brush—mainly willow thickets—comprise the remaining land areas, and the thickets are found mostly in low-lying riverine and flood-plain areas. Wetlands, in the form of small lakes (less than fifteen acres), ponds, swamps, and swales, cover roughly 5 percent of the land.

This is a typical southern Michigan farmland where the author conducted his study. Small crop fields interspersed with scattered woodlots, swales, ponds, and thickets constitute it's most important features. The relatively benign weather patterns and exceptionally high nutritional plane lend themselves to an ideal whitetail environment in which the control of their numbers is difficult

Throughout the township some large land tracts exist (from seventy- to one thousand-acre parcels), but in between there are numerous small holdings from lot-size parcels to plots of ten to fifteen acres. The human population is roughly twenty to twenty-two people per square mile. The deer population is roughly fifteen to twenty per square mile. Approximately 70 percent of the area is hunted; 30 percent is posted. Trespassing is very common and seems to be getting worse. Despite the posting of land there are few, if any, true sanctuaries for the deer because of this trespassing. Hunting pressure is moderate to high. Hunter densities, during the archery seasons, run from two or three per square mile on private areas, to ten or more on the state land. During the gun season they range from three to seven on the private lands to as high as fifteen to twenty per square mile on weekends on the state land. These are the conditions and circumstances under which the deer in this area live. To fully understand not only these deer, but any deer, this is the kind of qualifying data that must be known and often is not included even when scientists discuss deer behaviors.

Section I

The Life of a
White-Tailed Fawn

In southern Michigan approximately 80 percent to 85 percent of fawns are born in the week between June 1 and June 8. The pregnant doe selects a territory of five to ten acres as her birthing ground. The quality of the territory depends on her dominance ranking (largely a function of her age). The poorer or less diverse the herd's habitat or the lower the population density, the larger the birthing area will be.

Researchers generally believe that the doe does not attempt to birth in any particular spot within the limits of her birthing ground since births have been observed in thick cover and in the open. Most observers say that wherever the doe happens to be when it's her time is where she delivers. I don't agree with this. It seems to me that if we could observe enough live births, we'd probably be able to detect subtle differences, depending on the age and experience of the dams, that would account for some of the differences in birth locations, and differences in survival rates of fawns.

Many factors affect survival rates, including the severity of the previous winter, the weather in the early spring (i.e., the rapidity of spring green-up), the weather for the first week to ten days after the fawn is dropped, population density, the age-class distribution of does, the quality and type of habitat, and the number and type of predators present. I'll discuss each of these factors as they have an impact on fawn survival.

WEATHER-RELATED FACTORS

To have a good chance of survival, white-tailed fawns need to weigh between five and seven pounds at birth. If a fawn weighs more this is probably only to its benefit, although there is some evidence to indicate that obesity can be a problem too. The primary problem is that many weigh less. Small, weak fawns face serious obstacles. Some are so weak they can't stand to nurse; they'll die within hours.

This newborn buck fawn (notice the off-colored swirls of hair between his eyes and the bases of his ears; theses are the locations of his "pedicles," the platforms from which his future antlers will grow) is typical of newborns. He is alone but not "abandoned," as many people who find them assume. The best thing to do if you encounter such a fawn is to leave the area; his dam will return for him.

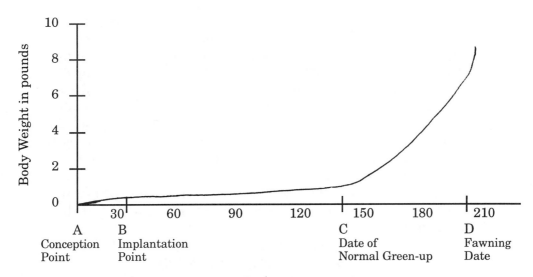

Figure 1.1 Fetal Growth Curve

Four points on the Fetal Growth Curve warrant elaboration:

Point A. Day 0 is the day (date) of conception. This varies by region (normally, but not always, by latitude). In southern Michigan it is thought to be between November 18 and November 25 for the vast majority (probably in excess of 95 percent) of all adult does. The remaining adult does and the majority of yearling (juvenile) does that will breed (greater than 60 percent) will cycle in and breed twenty-eight to thirty days later (December 16–25), while a lower percentage (less than 40 percent) will cycle in some twenty-eight to thirty days later still (January 13–20).

Point B. Represents the point at which implantation of the now-forming embryo occurs in the uterine wall (between December 20–25 in most adult does, and January or February in yearlings). This is the changeover point. Prior to implantation, the developing embryo had been deriving all its energy from the egg yolk; from implantation forward, all energy will be supplied from the dam.

Point C. A critical transition period. As mentioned in the text, "timing is everything!" Spring "green-up" should occur at this time (in southern Michigan), but is weather-dependent and thus variable; metabolic and developmental increases will occur since they're triggered by length of daylight (an annual constant). Because of this, the developmental health and well-being of both doe and fawn(s) are dependent upon Mother Nature cooperating as expected.

Point D. Gestation length varies by subspecies and nutritional plane, and runs approximately 190 to 220 days. In southern Michigan it is roughly 190 days. Approximately 90 percent of our fawns are born between May 28 and June 8 each year.

Fawns of yearling does have an especially tough time of it. Because of the does' inexperience, fawns of primipara does of any age are at risk—particularly in northern regions that experience hard winters. The bodies of yearling does are not yet fully developed and, because they're smaller and less dominant, they get less food, on average, than older does. If the food shortage is severe enough, many of their fetuses will abort or, if born, will arrive stillborn or badly malnourished. As many as 40 percent or more of the fawns of yearling does may be lost annually.

The last couple weeks of winter and the first couple weeks of what is normally spring determine the fate of thousands of fawns each year (see *Figure 1.1*).

If winter lingers, if the snows don't melt, if there's a severe late cold snap or a late winter/early spring freezing rain, thousands of deer can perish in a matter of days. Losses of this kind are always highest among the unborn, the young, the old, and the most dominant bucks. Even if winter's grip loosens and spring green-up is on time, if a fawn is unlucky enough to be born during a very cold or heavy rain, the fawn may die. Because newborn fawns have an extremely low ratio of body volume to surface area, they have little ability to retain heat. Cold—especially cold rain—can quickly sap them of any reserves they might have. Because of their metabolic and physiological limitations, they're quite vulnerable for the first couple weeks of their lives. Although I'm not aware of it ever happening in the northern regions, in arid sections of the country a late spring/early summer drought or extreme heat can also be a killer.

The good news? Even if winter weather was rough, if it breaks relatively early, the deer will generally recover very quickly.

POPULATION DENSITY

Despite its lush appearance in early summer, the natural world is not an unlimited supply house for deer. Deer are what biologists refer to as "selective feeders." Even a small deer population may feed so heavily on particular vegetation that it eradicates it altogether. Meanwhile, other types of vegetation may be seldom, if ever, touched because they offer no nutritional value for the deer. Because of this, deer have a tremendous impact on the growth and distribution patterns of flora in their habitat. The larger the deer population, the more profound the effect.

Biologists often list vegetative growth by category when describing what deer eat. Most commonly, they name three categories: preferred foods, secondary foods, and starvation foods. In reality, of course, there's simply a continuum extending from most desired (most beneficial) to least desired (of no nutritional value).

Although this juniper, or eastern red cedar, is not considered a "preferred species" by most authorities, in my study area it is heavily browsed even though deer numbers are comparatively low (twelve to twenty deer per square mile). Other less desirable species are seldom consumed until the more preferred foods diminish. Fertile habitats with mild weather and low deer numbers are conditions that lead to population explosion, among white-tailed deer.

Preferred Foods	Secondary Foods	Starvation Foods
white oak acorns	poplar	hemlock
alfalfa	willow	red pine
soybeans		
white cedar		

When deer are at low population density, the preferred foods are plentiful enough that rarely or only at certain times of year will foods of secondary choice need to be eaten. Under such circumstances, birth rates are invariably high and natural mortality exceedingly low—the ideal situation for a population explosion among the deer.

As the population grows, secondary foods become more and more utilized because preferred foods are increasingly difficult to find. In this situation, natural mortality increases somewhat, and replacement/recruitment (replacement is the substitution of one animal in the population for one that's been lost; recruitment is the number of fawns that survive to their first autumn) decreases as well.

As the population reaches or exceeds the habitat's carrying capacity, the deer must turn to starvation foods. The deer who cannot find enough foods of nutritive value to get them through will perish. But before they perish, they'll inflict terrible damage on the habitat, damage it may take years to recover from, if at all.

Before starvation on such a scale occurs, replacement ceases. Fawns are aborted, stillborn, or die at early ages. If conditions are severe enough, what can occur is a major die-off of adult deer plus the entire crop of fawns.

Habitats vary, of course, in their ability to support deer. Mixed or varied habitats are always more productive than monocultures. Diverse agricultural areas, like those of southern Michigan, are the best of all. But farmers will only tolerate so much damage to their crops, and insurance companies and public officials will tolerate only so many vehicle/deer accidents before they demand a reduction of the deer population. Michigan DNR biologists (and most other state biologists) by legislative mandate have only three reasons to justify deer herd reduction: damage to the habitat, damage to crops, and vehicle/deer accidents.

AGE-CLASS DISTRIBUTION

In human newborns and (rarely) in older infants there's a set of symptoms, always involving malnourishment, that physicians diagnose as "failure to thrive." According to Nelson (*Textbook of Pediatrics*): "Most instances of failure to thrive result from psychosocial circumstances, not always apparent, which adversely affect the child's intake, absorption, or utilization of food. Emotional deprivation and physical neglect or abuse, including withholding of food, are commonly associated." Such an etiology can be ascribed in the failure to thrive of whitetail fawns, especially those born to yearling does. Research shows that primipara (especially yearling primipara) does often do not make good dams. They may ignore their fawns or fail to feed them as often or as long as more experienced dams do their fawns. Some primipara does have been observed to walk away and abandon their fawns. Such "failure to mother" behaviors may result in as high as 40 percent mortality of the fawns born to primipara yearling dams. In herds that have been very heavily hunted the population may be skewed in favor of these younger dams; therefore, there could be an extremely high loss in the annual fawn crop as a result of this factor.

There is no truth to the myth of the "old dry doe." Does can and usually do bear and raise fawns every year until they die, especially in herds whose populations are well within the constraints of their habitat. The older the female cohorts, the more successful they will be in rearing their fawns to recruitment age (four to five months). Research indicates a wide array of variation, depending on location and habitat, but typical figures run from 40 percent or higher mortality rates for primipara does to about 7 percent for adult does aged four, five, or six. Obviously, the older the age-class distribution of does in a given herd, the higher will be the percentage of fawns recruited.

QUALITY AND TYPES OF HABITAT

Southern Michigan's agricultural lands, with their array of small grain crops, scattered woodlots, and riparian thickets, provide excellent habitats for the white-tailed deer. Most of

the Midwest offers equally good habitats, as do many locations in the East, Northeast, and Southeast. This pattern of
agricultural land, interspersed with cover, is probably the
reason we have more deer today in North America than
ever before. The unbroken, mature forests and unending
prairie grasslands the Europeans found on this continent
would always have supported some deer, but the habitats
were far from ideal for the whitetail. When we cleared land
for agriculture and timber, historically, we went overboard.
Almost all areas were totally denuded, even marginal land.
What we didn't clear intentionally was often destroyed by
wildfire roaring through the slash we left behind. In many
areas, therefore, it's only been in the last fifty to eighty
years that we have begun to have the ideal habitat so widely found today.

Many areas that historically were not particularly "friendly" for deer are
friendlier today despite their extremes in weather, because of mankind's elimi-
nation of predators and manipulation of habitats.

These habitats are so beneficial for deer that even in severe weather deer numbers are difficult to contain. Menominee County in Michigan's Upper Peninsula, for example, is heavily farmed in its southern half, and receives heavy snows and brutal cold in winter, but its high-energy crops and perfectly spaced cedar/poplar thickets provide everything the deer need to thrive. The same can be said for areas of Wisconsin, Minnesota, and the Canadian provinces of Alberta, Saskatchewan, and Manitoba. And in the past few years researchers have learned a lot about how to improve habitat conditions even further. So it is no surprise that departments of natural resources have a devil of a time keeping herds to manageable levels.

The situation in Michigan's U.P. is representative of these "deer-friendly" habitats. Forestry is the number one industry of the western U.P., supplying some 40 percent of the jobs and income. It only makes sense to coordinate the needs of forestry with those of wildlife. Fortunately, the whitetails' needs are not at odds with those of most other wildlife, and habitats are not manipulated for whitetails to the detriment of other animals—with the possible unfortunate exception of the wolf.

Following are some key points to keep in mind about the habitat manipulation of forested environments:

- Clear cuts need to be kept small, no more than fifty acres, whenever possible
- Strip cutting (long, narrow swaths less than three hundred feet wide) provides more usable area for whitetails than other cut configurations
- The largest number of small openings in the forest canopy (two to five acres each) is best
- Cuts within an enclosed area should be staggered over a period of years, if possible, to provide more forest openings and more opportunities for browsing/grazing on a continuing basis
- Softwoods should be cut during the winter months so that slash created also provides whitetails with food during the critical winter weather

This little "button buck" is fortunate to be alive; ten days before I took this photo he'd been attacked and bitten by a coyote (notice the raw wound on his rear right leg). I'd seen him the day of the attack. His leg was bleeding severely and he was so agitated I couldn't get anywhere near him. I saw him again approximately one week after this photo was taken and the wound was already healing. He looked fine, but I've not been able to identify him or perhaps haven't seen him since.

- In hardwood stands clear cuts should be avoided; selective cuts, taking only the largest, most valuable trees, will create the most openings in the forest canopy, promoting optimal space and sunlight for new growth while still providing cover and an ongoing mast crop
- Monocultural stands (single tree species) should not be planted if possible. If unavoidable, they should be interspersed with other types of vegetation

The objective in all these practices is to promote as diverse a habitat as possible in a forested environment. Since these techniques also afford better disease control and fire protection for the trees, they benefit both forestry and wildlife.

POPULATION LEVELS AND TYPES OF PREDATORS

Coyotes. According to research, coyotes, being carrion eaters, are more likely to be scavengers of whitetails than predators (Knowlton 1964; Niebauer and Rongstad 1977). Ozoga & Harger (1966) determined that coyotes killed few whitetails other than fawns that were under two months of age. Does have been observed chasing coyotes away from their fawns. Nonetheless, other studies have found that the removal of coyotes from an area leads to greater survival of fawns—up to 40 percent greater in some cases! What these studies did not take into account, however, is that coyote-induced mortality may be compensatory and therefore of less significance than it might seem.

What most experts agree on is that the degree of coyote predation varies widely from region to region and is influenced by several factors. The ratio of coyote to deer is important. The more coyotes there are in relation to deer numbers, the more likely they will be predatory. Habitat is also important; coyotes are more effective hunters in open cover than in forested or mixed environments. In addition, the fewer alternative food sources available to the coyotes, the more likely they will attempt to hunt whitetails, and the more attempts they make, the better they'll get at it. Finally, the presence of other whitetail predators will lower the overall deer:predator ratio, giving all predators a greater advantage over the deer.

Bobcats. Even more of a deer scavenger than the coyote, nonetheless the bobcat accounts for some fawn mortality for essentially the same reasons outlined above for the coyote. In the northern reaches of the whitetails' range, bobcats and lynxes undoubtedly claim some deer in yards; however, most, if not all, of this is compensatory. The predatory impact of bobcats is quite insignificant overall, especially in southern Michigan, where bobcats are practically nonexistent.

Mountain lions. There are no mountain lions in southern Michigan. Research by Hornacker in 1970 in Idaho, however, suggests that mountain lions could have a significant impact where the ratio of lion to deer is high enough. Finding ratios that varied from 1:135 to 1:201, Hornacker concluded that even though the lions were killing an average of thirteen to twenty deer annually, they were not limiting the deer population at those ratios. It's unlikely that there is any place in recent times with a ratio high enough for mountain lions to limit deer numbers despite their obvious predatory efficiency.

Bears. Despite their power and size, bears are very poor predators. Though they unquestionably account for some small degree of fawn mortality, they are deer scavengers, not predators. In recent times, there are no bears in southern Michigan.

Domestic dogs. The predatory impact of dogs on deer is a hotly debated issue. Forbes et al. (1971) concluded that five hundred to one thousand deer are killed by dogs annually in Pennsylvania. In Arkansas, Segelquist et al. (1969) concluded that heavy parasite loads could make deer more vulnerable to dogs; however, many other authorities in various places throughout the country have concluded that dogs impose only a minor threat to deer.

I believe they do have an impact on Michigan's deer, but only on a sporadic, localized basis. I've seen dogs running deer on numerous occasions. In the late winter of 1984, I witnessed a dog kill a deer. I believe their greatest threat is to fawns and, in the North, to winter-weakened deer. It's important to realize that dogs and other predators do not need to catch a deer to be responsible for its death. Stress induced by the chase may lead to death from exhaustion at a later point.

Wolves. According to studies by David Mech et al. (1970, 1974, 1977, 1981), wolves constitute the primary source of natural mortality for deer in conterminous range. Perhaps wolves affected deer populations historically, but today's wolf populations are so low and so localized (and wolf:deer ratios are so skewed) that their impact is minimal. There are no wolves in southern Michigan. This very issue is, of course, being hotly debated right now in our western states as the government is reintroducing wolves into some of their historical range.

In sum, with so few predators throughout much of the whitetails' range and considering their overall predatory inefficiency, most deer populations are not limited by predation to any significant degree. The only possible exception to that today is by coyotes in the arid Southwest. It's also true that if a few deer are taken by predators, a herd will have fewer mouths to feed and, paradoxically, the remaining deer may actually be better off for it.

These habitat and predator factors are crucial for survival of the fawns and of the herd itself. Actually, game-management people do not usually concern themselves with how many fawns are born; rather, they speak of "recruitment rates," that is, how many fawns survive until autumn of their first year. After recruitment age, survival rates are not significantly different from those of yearlings or adults.

Of course there's much more to a fawn's life than just mortality and survival. For the first couple weeks of life, a fawn may sleep as much as twenty hours a day. Its dam will nurse it, on average, four or five times each day. Even if it is one of a pair of newborns, the fawn will bed alone for the first couple weeks of its life.

I've often photographed fawns during the first few days after birth. The natural reaction of a fawn for its first ten days or so is to freeze in the face of any potentially dangerous situation. Because of their spotted coats, they're surprisingly difficult to see. The fawn's white spots give it an appearance very similar to dappled sunlight shining onto the forest floor. At least that is what is widely said. I believe there's more to it. I've often found fawns along grassy edges or in open fields or in semiopen brush where their coats would not afford very effective camouflage. What I think is more to the point is that it's very hard to spot an animal that's not moving, and fawns do that very well! When not with their dams, they'll curl up with their necks extended or tucked and lay their heads flat on the ground. If approached, they will not move. It's well-documented that fawns exude very little odor; well-trained hunting dogs have on many occasions passed within feet of them without detecting them, and it is believed their natural predators often do the same.

After ten days of age, if you approach too closely, there will be a sudden blur of motion as the long-legged fawn dashes for cover. Within two days after birth fawns are capable of outrunning a human; within ten days, most dogs —and even coyotes and bobcats—would lose them. At the "twixt and tween" stage of perhaps eight to twelve days, one will occasionally encounter some rather unusual behavior. Annette and I were on vacation with our boys a few years ago in the Black Hills of South Dakota in an area with many whitetails. While driving through Custer State Park, I just happened to spot a fawn lying curled up fifty or sixty feet away on a wooded slope. We parked quickly, grabbed a camera, and approached quietly. The fawn, curled up at the base of a ponderosa pine, saw us but didn't move. I took a couple shots from roughly twenty feet, then moved a few feet closer. The fawn bolted. His problem was that there was a windfall right beside him, the bottom of which cleared the ground by only a couple of inches. The fawn couldn't jump over it, so he tried to go under it. He couldn't do that either, so he was trapped with his little head under the log and his back end up in the air, trying his darnedest to run and, of course, getting nowhere. It was a very humorous sight, but if we had been a coyote searching for an easy meal, his panic and confusion would surely have cost him his life.

When fawns become separated from their dams, they'll locate one another by means of vocalizations, as well as by sighting. The fawn bleats to call its dam. The bleat sounds very similar to that of a young calf, only softer. The doe, in turn, makes a soft, almost catlike mewing sound. She mews repeatedly as she wanders into the area where she last saw the fawn. Upon hearing its dam, the fawn will respond immediately by running to her.

A young fawn grows very rapidly. In two weeks it doubles its weight. Two weeks later it doubles its weight again, and by early September it will weigh roughly fifty pounds. By a month of age fawns are beginning to eat solid foods, feeding both with the dam and, to some extent, on their own. They'll mimic their dam but they'll also experiment by trial and error.

Like human babies, fawns seem to sleep and rest all the time, as if revving up their engines for the bursts of energy that will be displayed later. When I was a young biology student, it was almost sacrilege to speak of animal behavior as "play." It was thought that play was a frivolous form of expression that no animal other than humans could ever afford, but then something revolutionary happened. Psychologists, psychiatrists, and then animal behaviorists began to speak of play as "the work of childhood." No one could watch fawns during the summer months for more than a few moments and not know they are playing. They cavort with each other, jump over each other, chase their dams, chase a piece of paper caught in the wind, chase other animals, and so on.

Fawns are very much "full of themselves," and they expend a tremendous amount of energy. But this is not idle, meaningless activity; such behavior builds strength, stamina, coordination, and a realistic appreciation of the bounds of their physical limitations. Their heightened physical abilities and their knowledge of themselves and their habitat can save their lives in dangerous circumstances.

The fawns' exuberance is sometimes contagious. You'll sometimes see their dams, aunts, older siblings, and especially their cousins getting involved in raucous goings-on. Such behavior never lasts long—except when it involves same-aged cousins—and I've never seen it except in summer. Older deer never behave this way unless it is in the presence of fawns, who are the instigators. No observer can fail to realize that the play which is the hallmark of human children is a big part of the whitetails' world as well.

2

The Life of a
White-Tailed Buck

It makes sense to begin a discussion of the buck's life cycle when he's somewhat less than one year old—in mid-May for most yearlings—because that is when life as he has known it changes drastically. Since his birth, the buck has essentially never been separated from his dam. In mid-May, however, adult does separate themselves from the rest of the herd a couple weeks before giving birth to their new fawns. The dam actually runs off her young buck, often by a series of physically aggressive acts carried out over a period of hours. Of course, the buck is totally confused and bewildered. His dam has never behaved this way before. Even if he is with a brother or sister, he feels very much lost. Such fawns are easy to spot, and they're extremely vulnerable.

In mid-May of 1992, while doing my daily survey, I kept seeing a pair of fawns just south of my house. For more than three weeks I saw these deer practically every day. These two repeatedly behaved in a manner that would only be considered normal for whitetails of this age. They were so unobservant that on several occasions I walked right up to them in the open before they knew I was there. They spent a great deal of their time in the open, where they were totally exposed. Even when aware of my presence, they'd run off a short distance and, even though I was still in the area, they'd return, only to run off again.

In mid-May of 1993 my wife, Annette, and I saw another pair of fawns behaving in a similar fashion. This pair, however, were inclined to hang around a couple heavily used roadways. We saw this same pair for weeks, day in and day out. They were clearly at great risk for traffic accidents.

For many years the records of the Michigan State Police have shown that deer/vehicle accidents do not occur with equal frequency throughout the year. There are three periods of time when they're most likely to happen: the last week of October to mid-November, late March to mid-April, and mid-May to mid-June.

These records must have been very perplexing to early observers, but now we know why they wax and wane this way. In October to November rut-driven frenzied behaviors are responsible for the increase in accidents; in March to April the frenetic behaviors of early spring are responsible; and in mid-May to June it is invariably the yearling deer, forced to care for themselves for the first time in a dangerous world, that get killed on our highways.

As traumatic as the fawns' separation from the dams must be, they gradually calm down and adjust. By early to mid-June most of their dangerously disoriented behavior has subsided. The bond between the buck and his dam will never be the same again. The buck at this time apparently experiences a desire to wander. He shows a drive to strike out on his own or, at least, apart from his dam. He may wander for many miles and then return in a matter of days. Then he'll strike out again. Each time, the bonds to his maternal family and his first home territory become increasingly weakened. This separation, both physical and psychological, may take several weeks or several months.

Female fawns do not normally experience this psychological and physical isolation as a result of the separation from their dams, judging from their behavior.

In his wanderings, the yearling buck meets up with other bucks. He will probably end up as a member of a bachelor group. With yearlings, this transition is very gradual. He may meet up with another yearling and drift with him for a while. He may stay with a certain buck or group of bucks for a few days and then wander off again by himself. He may drift from one bachelor group to another for much of the summer. A few yearling bucks remain alone or on the fringes of a group without ever becoming real members.

Bachelor groupings are extremely tenuous, at least in my study area. More often than not I see late spring, summer and early autumn bucks alone, not as members of associated buck groups.

During his second summer the yearling buck is growing his first set of antlers. By mid-September the antlers will harden and he will shed their velvet covering.

From every point of view, physically, behaviorally, and psychologically, the young buck is now the equivalent of a "teen-ager." Like human teen-agers, he feels awkward and ill at ease. He doesn't quite fit in, doesn't quite understand the changes that are occurring in his life. He looks once again as if he feels alienated, as when he was abandoned by his dam the previous spring.

In October, the buck group splinters, if not physically, at least psychologically. If the bucks are still hanging out together, they are cantankerous with each other. They spar constantly. The really dominant bucks continually run off the younger ones. Every other buck, it seems, wants to test him. It's no fun being "low man on the totem pole," and the young buck doesn't yet understand what is happening to him.

Yearling bucks are physically capable of breeding, but they may or may not be capable psychologically. If they're severely dominated by older bucks, they are unlikely to be capable of asserting themselves sufficiently to breed. This is most likely in populations having healthy age-class distributions.

In addition, there are bucks that, for whatever reason, choose not to leave their dam's maternal family. In a normal herd, these bucks will not breed at all and have been called "psychological castrates." But in a herd that has been heavily harvested—80 percent to 90 percent of the bucks have been culled—the losses will result in a very poor age-class distribution (a majority of the bucks being in the younger age groups). These bucks may then be forced into breeding roles, especially if they are dominant (physically stronger and more aggressive) among their age mates. This is a situation common to states with "buck-only" hunting regulations.

Even if he is not dominant, the yearling buck will still be very interested in the breeding-related activities that are going on around him, but rather than imitating, he will become agitated and hyperactive. During October and early November, dominant bucks channel their energies into sparring, rubbing, scraping, and domineering the other

This is a tragic loss! A two-year-old buck forced into an active breeding role because of a lack of any truly dominant bucks in the herd is commonplace in many regions with "traditional" deer management practices. Even under the best management schemes very few bucks live long enough to become dominant. Under systems such as Michigan's, far fewer than 1 percent of our bucks ever live to three years or older. This means that immature bucks, such as this one, become dominant breeders as two-year-olds, and it often costs them their lives. Despite claims to the contrary, the DNR does not know the long-term effects that this will have upon our deer.

bucks in the area. These stereotyped behaviors are the pre-rut rituals about which much has been written. The younger or dominated bucks have no such outlet—or at least, it is not such an effective mechanism of release for them. These bucks tend to channel their energies into incautious physical motion—motion that often gets them killed!

Too often we speak of deer behavior as if every deer behaves exactly like every other. This is definitely not the case. My family has three cats. Each cat has a distinct personality. In the way each interacts with the others, spends its time, reacts to food or to various family members each is different, unique. Deer are different from one another, too.

To be sure, there are commonalities of behavior. We can speak of tendencies, patterns, probabilities, but we should never be so arrogant as to believe we can speak with certainty when referring to the behaviors of a particular animal. To do so is to ignore the diversity found in every species.

Researchers have found that during the prerut period some bucks are good sign makers, making hundreds of rubs and as many as fifty or more scrapes. Other bucks are not good sign makers. It's well established that as a buck matures his sign-making abilities and behaviors generally increase. It's thus believed that the majority of sign making in any given area is done by the most dominant buck(s) in that area. However, there's also reason to believe there are some bucks that, for whatever reason, will never be good sign makers.

Some generalities do seem to hold true. For example, the more dominant the animal, the better sign maker he will be. Even within the younger age classes the more dominant animals will be the most active sign makers. Recently, trophy hunters (not researchers, so far as I know) have begun to speak of the "unhuntable buck." They believe that for some reason certain bucks rub and scrape very little, if at all, and never in a logical, predictable manner. Because they do not show patterns, none of the usual hunting tactics will work on them. I can't prove it, but I believe such bucks do exist.

Also, the more balanced the herd, i.e., the closer the buck:doe ratio is to 1:1, the more sign-making activity there will be. The more skewed this ratio, the more sign making diminishes. In a herd, for example, where the ratio is 1:3, there will be less sign than in a 1:1 herd; in a 1:10 herd, there will be even less. Finally, the better the age-class distribution, i.e., the larger the percentage of older animals, the more sign making there will be. If 80 percent to 90 percent of a herd's legally antlered bucks are killed year in and year out, this will skew the ratio markedly. These factors are key to quality deer management and quality deer hunting, both of which I'll discuss in Chapter 8.

If a yearling buck survives his first autumn, in some regions of the country he then stands a good chance of growing to maturity, becoming dominant, and contributing his genetic potential to the herd.

ANTLER CYCLE AND GROWTH

Newborn buck fawns can be recognized by swirls of darker colored hair growing over the area of their skulls where their antlers will grow later in life. During their first summer, buck fawns begin growing thickened, raised, bony platforms on their frontal skull plates. By early autumn these raised areas, called "pedicles," will be one-half to one inch tall and one-half to three-quarter inch in diameter. Pedicles produce a noticeable bump on top of the head of the buck, now known as a "button buck." At this point, antler-related growth stops for the year.

Each early spring, usually early May, the buck will begin his annual antler-growing cycle. The growth is at first stimulated by photoperiodism (the length of daylight), later by hormonal secretion. Antler growth begins on the buck's pedicles. A skinlike layer first grows over the pedicles, completely covering them. Scientists call this skin layer "velvet." It's a rich matrix of blood vessels that deposit for the next four to five months all the nutrients, mostly calcium and phosphorous, needed for antler growth.

Recent research indicates that it may well be the smaller of these two yearling bucks that eventually (at maturity, if either lives that long) becomes the most dominant, with the largest set of antlers.

For each buck the size of his antlers in any given year is determined by his age, nutritional plane, and physiological status, and by his genetics. Healthy bucks grow bigger antlers than ill, injured, or diseased ones. The overall shape and symmetry (conformation) of his antlers is determined by his genetics.

For years we've been told that "spike" bucks were genetically inferior animals, but around 1980 Lou Verme, a pioneer in whitetail research, told me that that was ridiculous. Lou told me that German researchers in the 1920s and '30s did some work on European stags, but no one in this country paid much attention. The Germans proved, at least to their satisfaction, that spikes were not inferior animals, just ill-fed animals. The German research concluded that if you control the herd, balance it with the ability of the habitat to support it, the spikes will grow antlers capable of matching any. Poor nutrition, they said, not inferior genetics, produces spikes.

In the intervening years American research has found that Dr. Verme was essentially correct. In the March 1994 *Deer & Deer Hunting* magazine, Larry L. Weishuhn wrote, "I now believe there are two main reasons for spikes: late-born fawns and poor nutrition." He added, "I believe genetics are a minor player in the spike question." This is a man who has done as much research on spikes as anyone, and he ought to know.

The major factors that determine antler growth are age, nutritional plane, physiological status, genetics, and minerals.

AGE

Yearling bucks can grow antlers that range from small, sublegal spikes to small ten-point racks. As mentioned above, research indicates that late-born fawns can grow spikes. If a doe fawn comes into estrous in her first autumn and is bred, it happens one or two months (in the Deep South, perhaps even three months) after the bulk of the doe herd has been bred, so the subsequent birthing by such a doe will be correspondingly later than other births. Late breeding is not at all uncommon.

Primipara does usually give birth to single fawns, rather than twins, as multipara does do. If the buck fawn's dam is one of these late-bred does, the buck will almost invariably grow spikes as a yearling, no matter what his nutritional plane or his genetics. And, since primapara does birth a larger number of buck fawns than doe fawns, it is this segment of the doe population from which many of our spike-horn bucks spring. When a buck consumes food, all the resulting energy is first channeled toward growth and development. This is the top priority. Any energy left over then goes toward antler growth.

As yearlings these late-born bucks have bodies that are still underdeveloped and require much more energy for normal growth than do those of yearling bucks born earlier. There is simply not enough nutritional energy left over for sizable antlers in these younger animals. Interestingly, however, research now shows that by the time these animals are two, three, or four years old they have usually caught up to their earlier-born cohorts and may even surpass them in antler mass.

Even more surprisingly, the biggest adult bucks generally turn out to have been the modest-size yearlings, not the biggest. The modest fours, sixes, and small eights seem to grow bigger antlers as mature bucks than do the big eights and small tens of the yearling class. Undoubtedly, research into the cause of this will continue.

In any event, yearlings can never under any circumstances grow the truly immense antlers of mature bucks. They'll never have the same mass, tine length, and spread of bucks three, four, and five years old. Generally speaking, two-year-olds will grow bigger antlers than yearlings.

Each year until five or six years of age a buck's antlers should increase in size. After that, they'll stay about the same size until his teeth and/or physical health deteriorate, at which time his antler size will decrease. Bucks seldom live beyond ten or eleven years, and even in herds managed for quality, only a very low percentage of bucks live to full maturity (four years or older).

NUTRITIONAL PLANE

When I mentioned above that the body-growth needs of the buck come first, antler development second, I told only part of the story. Nutritional availability fluctuates dramatically throughout the year, as does the deer's ability to handle these changes and minimize their impact. There's frequently a nutritional bottleneck in the northern reaches of the whitetails' range in winter. Usually, spring's riches quickly restore their vitality, and the deer flourish, showing normal antler growth. Sometimes, however, this bottleneck is so severe that thousands of animals perish, and tens of thousands more come through in such emaciated condition that it takes many weeks of high-quality, protein-rich foodstuffs for them to regain their lost weight.

This kind of severely debilitated state and its prolonged recovery period will most profoundly affect the young, as well as the most dominant bucks, who entered the winter period severely weakened as a result of their heavy breeding activity in the fall (the price they pay for dominance). Thus antler mass may be reduced among the most dominant bucks the following year. In our western states, especially in the Southwest, drought conditions can reek havoc in much the same way.

If winter's bottleneck was not too severe but the availability of spring food is reduced by a severe late frost, prolonged spring snows, or prolonged cold spring rain, the nutritional decline can be quite profound. In winter, a deer's metabolism slows down, reducing his nutritional requirements; but in the spring metabolic rates rise, and so do nutritional needs. Deprivation in spring is not as easily overcome as a winter deprivation, and it can be even more costly in terms of antler development.

Throughout much of North America summer nutrition is not a problem for deer, but it can be in the arid Southwest. If it's too dry or too hot, the consequences can be dire, even fatal, but they do not normally affect antler development quite as dramatically since they take place near the end of the antler growth period, in late summer.

There's a factor that can impact antler development that I've seldom seen written up or heard discussed. When bucks are sporting polished antlers and their hormones are surging (from mid-September to late December), they're kings of the hill. All other deer are submissive to them. Hunters who only see deer during the autumn and others who do not observe deer closely may be unaware that at other times bucks are very passive. When the bucks' hormones diminish and they've cast their antlers, or are in the velvet (antler growing) period, females clearly run the show. A dominant old matriarch will often bully them. Perhaps that's why bucks usually stay away from doe groups. Except for aggressive acts associated with breeding, I've never seen bucks—even dominant ones—that were not deferential toward does, giving them the best feeding sites. If food is scarce enough, this could affect antler development.

What this points to is the crucial importance of maintaining deer herds within the constraints of the carrying capacity of their habitat. When carrying capacity is exceeded, for whatever reason, the deer pay a severe price ranging from decreased antler mass and fawn loss to winter starvation and death, and the habitat is destroyed for future generations.

One of the most reliable indicators of the state of the deer herd in relation to carrying capacity is the growth or decline in the diameter of basal antler measurements in yearling bucks. A decrease in these measurements foretells an increasing herd and/or a declining capacity. In either case, if the health and well-being of the herd is to be maintained, the herd must be reduced or the habitat improved.

PHYSIOLOGICAL STATUS

A buck's health affects his antler development. If he's injured, ill, diseased, carrying a heavy parasite load, or weakened by a poor or damaged habitat, antler mass will be decreased. Because they affect physiological well-being, there's every reason to believe that high population density, severe domination by other deer, or severe predatory harassment will affect antler development, too.

Injury, illness, and disease are common in deer. Leg injuries seem to be among the most frequent. During my three-year study, I saw two deer that I knew had broken legs, and a third, which clearly had a leg that had been broken and healed, was killed by a neighbor. I also saw at least eight or nine others with clear leg injuries and a spike buck with a hind leg from the hock joint down entirely missing! Writing in *Deer & Deer Hunting* magazine (September 1991), Pat Durkin told of an eleven-year-old buck that had to be put down by a veterinarian. An autopsy revealed "heart disease, arthritis, foot rot, skin cuts, hair balls, malnutrition, skin infections, internal and external parasites, and hair and tooth loss." This buck had been living on a four-thousand acre breeding farm in Virginia, owned by the Smithsonian Institution, presumably a pretty cushy habitat. The title of the article was "Old Age Is No Friend." Ain't it the truth! Dr. Valerius Geist, a professor at The University of Calgary doing research on deer injuries, determined that "on average, bucks have to deal with twenty to thirty injury wounds per year!"

Physiological stress not only affects total antler mass, it also dictates when antlers will be cast. If a buck is healthy and vigorous (if he went into winter in pretty good shape) and has a high nutritional plane, he will retain his antlers longer than one that's weakened.

I saw a buck on southern Michigan agricultural land as late as March 13 that still had antlers. That was a six- or eight-point buck with what I estimated to be a fourteen- to sixteen-inch inside spread. One of the most humorous things I witnessed during my study occurred on February 27, 1992. I crested a hill overlooking a brushy area where I had frequently observed deer bedding in a corner of the brush, protected from the wind and exposed to the sun. Often they lie immediately next to the wire fenceline there. As soon as I crested the hill, I saw a doe jump the fence. Believing it probably wasn't alone, I focused my binoculars on the brush. Immediately I saw a buck lying tight against the fence. In his haste to exit, he didn't clear the fence; his antlers hung up in the wire, though his body catapulted over. Lying flat on his back he began thrashing his head from side to side. Finally he extricated himself, jumped up and ran away with both antlers still in place. He looked like a six-point with perhaps a twelve-inch inside spread.

GENETICS

Although I've mentioned that we now know that spike bucks are not the genetically inferior animals once thought, it is nonetheless a mistake to believe that genetics do not contribute to antler growth. Genetics affect at least three aspects of antler growth: maximum growth, symmetry and conformation, and the dam's contribution to antler mass.

Nutritional researchers have told us for a long time now that a protein-rich diet of 14 percent to 16 percent is essential for a buck to reach his maximum potential. Recent research, however, shows that bucks on such a diet grow antlers no larger than those kept on only 8 percent protein.

I believe that what research will ultimately prove is that there is a maximum growth potential that is very nearly identical for every buck within a subspecies. If the buck receives an adequate diet and lives long enough, he will reach that potential by way of many different nutritional paths. Think of how many hundreds of thousands—possibly reaching to the millions—of whitetails have been taken in the past century. A list of the Top Ten Heads of all time would show a variation of only a few inches of total mass. Quite often it's only a matter of fractions of an inch that separate the biggest bucks in each subspecies. Remember, this is a fraction of an inch out of a total mass of perhaps two hundred or, in cases of atypical heads, three hundred inches. The top heads seem to me to show clearly that there is a cap on antler mass and that we've been seeing it for some time now.

There are all kinds of antlers grown by whitetails. There are picture-perfect "basket-shaped" bucks with long main beams that sweep around close together over the nose, sporting high, inward-leaning tines. There are bucks with exceptionally wide, flaring, flat racks. And there are atypicals, with convoluted beams—sometimes grotesquely so—and multitudes of drop and sticker points going this way and that. With the exception of injury-related antler deformity, what's amazing is that whatever shape and symmetry a buck's rack takes this year, it'll take next year and the

This buck shows all the ingredients needed to become a truly magnificent specimen. Notice the long-legged-race-horse appearance, the chest deeper than the belly, and the lack of well-muscled neck and legs, all signs indicating a two-and-a-half-year-old animal. He won't be "prime" for at least two more years—if he survives—but imagine his potential.

year after that. They'll change in size and total mass each year, they'll change in number of points, but until the buck's health begins to decline, the conformational component is a constant.

I am astonished that even today the doe's role in antler development is seldom recognized by writers in the popular press. Even some deer management people apparently don't see it. We've moved bucks from the North, from Texas, from Montana to here and there in order to "inject" big buck genes into areas that have stunted deer—massive herds of stunted deer—living on old, decaying habitat incapable of supporting half of what they hold. What we've hoped for is a magic fix, but it's never worked. Never has, never will. Scientists have long realized the futility of such heroics, but their warnings have usually fallen on deaf ears.

It's just nuts to speak of a buck's passing along his genetic potential and ignoring that of the doe. Research shows that some does consistently yield sons with good antler growth, and some does do not. There are many questions on this subject left unanswered; probably the biggest and most difficult is, if we determine that some does are superior in their genetic contribution, could—and should—we manage for it? If we have the best interests of our deer herds in mind, who would say that antler growth, no matter how spectacular, is more important than the health of the herd? I believe we should work toward improving habitats, not fooling with genetics. If we do achieve genetic technological breakthroughs, I hope they will not be applied to the goal of increasing antler mass for the self-centered gratification of humans.

MINERALS

There is no question minerals play a part—under the heading of overall nutrition—but I believe too much is made of their importance. I question the often-made assertion that there are many and vast locations where mineral scarcity prevents maximum antler development. That's ridiculous. If mineral and nutritional levels in an area are high enough to grow healthy, mature, well-muscled deer, they are also high enough to produce healthy, well-formed antlers. If the overall nutrition of an area is adequate, the deer will obtain sufficient minerals to produce maximum antler growth. People who claim otherwise are, most generally, people who have a product to sell to gullible consumers.

3

The Life of a
White-Tailed Doe

Like the yearling buck, the yearling doe is confused when
run off by her dam, but she learns to adjust more quickly
than her brother, and by early June she spends the bulk of
her time along the perimeter of the area where her dam and
newborn half-siblings are. By the time the new fawns are
three or four weeks old, she will probably spend some time
in close association with them and her dam. The yearling's
relationship with her dam will never be as close as it was
before. The separation she experienced in mid-May has
forced her to become more alert and capable on her own, a
situation she now comes to accept. Whitetail society is
essentially matriarchal; females are much more strongly
bonded together than are the males, whose relationships
and groups show more tenuous bonds.

   The dam's family unit will normally continue to be the
family unit of the doe, but this is not always the case. Radio
telemetry studies and my own personal observations lead
me to believe that it's not all that uncommon for does to
wander into new territory. The telemetry studies indicate

such movements usually, but certainly not always, occur among yearling does.

I work at a hospital within the boundaries of a populous city. The hospital grounds, roughly a hundred acres, consist of an isolated hardwood lot, some planted pines, and several fallow fields. Other undeveloped properties surround the hospital property, sprawling north for perhaps a half mile. Surrounding all of this are numerous smaller cities and highly developed townships, running in all directions for several miles. There are countless highways, subdivisions, schools, factories, and seemingly wall-to-wall people, cars, and trucks.

Despite this, on four separate occasions in the past five or six years I've seen deer on the hospital grounds. It's hard to imagine how many backyards, dogs, cars, and people the deer had to circumvent to get there—and perhaps even harder to imagine why they would—but clearly new territories are getting populated this way, just as they have for many, many years.

While it's much more common for bucks to develop wanderlust, it's certainly not unheard of for does to wander off from their home range as well. It seems to occur most often at one of two times during the doe's life: either as a yearling, or as a much older adult if she loses her dominance ranking.

Two of the four sightings were single animals, one a buck, one a doe. Both were probably yearlings. The second time it was a buck and a doe together, and the last time it was a doe and two fawns. It's very clear that sometimes does can also get the wanderlust so typical of bucks.

As I've mentioned, it's not uncommon for yearling does to be pregnant—in southern Michigan, and many other regions of the whitetails' range, as many as 40 percent of yearling does are bred. Rates of pregnancy for yearlings elsewhere range from rare to 45 percent, depending on the herd, habitat, and weather.

Fawns of yearling does will usually be delivered around July first, perhaps even as late as September first, especially in the South. More than 85 percent of the time primipara does give birth to single fawns, as opposed to multipara does (ones who have given birth before), which more than 80 percent of the time give birth to twins. About 5 percent to 10 percent of the time multipara does have triplets, most frequently in areas of good habitat with low deer densities.

If the yearling doe is pregnant, she'll separate herself from the other deer, just as her dam did, and she'll select an unoccupied location for her birthing area.

This is the only time you'll ever see a whitetail behave truly territorially: she'll run off any other deer that invade her space. Incidentally, only whitetail does act this way. Until the time her fawn is roughly a month old she'll seldom leave the confines of her territory—and even then, only for short periods to feed or water. During these brief forays she may or may not meet up with others of her family unit.

Now ranking in the matriarchal group plays a more visible role than usual. If there is a high-population density, the yearling will be relegated to a pretty poor location for birthing; consequently her fawn may not survive. As many as 60 percent of fawns born to yearling does perish each year. Sometimes an entire crop may be lost through a variety of causes: neglect of fawns by inexperienced dams, poor nutrition, severe weather, predation, and so forth.

By the time the fawn is a month old, fawn and dam will leave the birthing area to join the maternal group, consisting of the fawn's aunts and cousins. These groups are relatively fluid; i.e., the various relatives come and go, interacting with two, three, or more subgroups within the territory where they live. Occasionally territories overlap, but interactions between members of unrelated groups are minimal compared with interactions between related deer. The size of a group ranges from four or five to perhaps as many as ten or fifteen. Size will depend on overall deer density, age-class distribution, condition of the habitat, and time of the year.

In summer most of the time is spent resting in the most shaded (coolest) locations and in heavy feeding. For nursing dams lactation is physiologically taxing, at least for the first six weeks or so. By late summer/early autumn the fawn has become a functioning ruminant and can be weaned. But even if it is still nursing, this will be far less draining on the dam than it was earlier.

Like bucks, does really gain weight now, beginning to accumulate fat deposits through a process called lipogenesis, which will help sustain them through winter. Between August and late October, body weight increases as much as 20 percent or even 25 percent. For yearlings, this percentage is probably even higher. Adult does (in southern Michigan) typically enter the late autumn period weighing from 110 to 130 pounds or more.

The disruptions caused by hunting and poaching (see Chapters 9 and 10) impact on bucks much more than on does, but doe behavior is affected, too. Beginning in late September and early October, does become more cautious and more nocturnal, lingering longer in the shadows and not venturing as far into the open as they did quite brazenly all summer. Also, the increased activity level and agitated behaviors of the bucks undoubtedly have a stimulating effect on the does.

As a doe approaches estrus, she becomes increasingly restless. Beginning in late October the bucks begin chasing does, checking them frequently to find one that has come into estrus. In this period the bucks follow several hundred feet behind any doe they believe may be receptive, or "hot." Prior to estrus, the doe does not allow the buck to catch her. After following her for a while, the buck loses interest and goes off looking for a more receptive doe.

At this point the bucks' hierarchy is most evident. If there is more than one buck chasing a doe, the bucks will

actually line up in clear order of dominance, the most dominant nearest the doe. Other bucks position themselves, single file, at a respectable distance of a hundred feet or more.
This period has been called "the chase phase" of the rut. As
the days pass, this behavior of the bucks becomes more and
more frenzied. If a doe voids, the buck smells her urine and,
it is believed, determines in this way if the doe is ready.
This is also when bucks "lip curl" or "Flehmen," as it's
called. When they stop to test the urine they do so using
what are apparently two separate sensory systems. One, of
course, is through the nose and involves the olfactory or
nasal system we're familiar with, and the other involves
what's been called the "vomeronasal" system. Researchers
Karl Miller and Larry Marchinton believe that the two systems function independently. The vomeronasal system consists of a small hole in the roof of a deer's mouth (Jacobson's
organ). The nerve endings from this organ go to a separate
portion of the deer's brain than those of the nasal, or olfactory, epithelium. No one knows for certain the exact role, or
roles, of the vomeronasal system, but we know it's used to
test the does' level of breeding readiness. It's when the buck
does so that we say he's "Flehmening." What he's actually
doing is sensing the receptive state of the doe by tasting her
urine and thus determining her condition. There's stereotypical posturing involved in this procedure; the buck raises
his head with his neck lowered or extended and he curls
back his upper lip. It is a practice common to all bucks at
this time. When the doe is ready to breed, she'll actively go
seeking the buck she desires if he's not already in attendance. She knows where to look for him by the sign he's created for the past several weeks in her territory.

Radio telemetry studies show that a receptive but unat-
tended doe will increase her activity level as much as twentyfold, or more, during the twelve to twenty-four hours
immediately prior to her cycling in. We now know that, in
her active seeking out of the buck, the doe contributes to
the rubs and scrapes traditionally considered "buck sign."

Wildlife researcher Grant Woods from Clemson
University has recorded data which show that does rub and

This buck is "Flehmening." Biologists believe that through this process of tasting and then inhaling the doe's urine, the buck actually becomes "primed" for future breeding behaviors. The entire sequence, for both bucks and does, is a very complex interaction of stimulus and response, behavioral and physiological, and serves to stimulate changes in all other deer as well. This, in a well-balanced herd, accomplishes many things. It ensures that all the "breeders" will be on the same page, so to speak, and it suppresses wasted breeding behaviors among younger animals, thus allowing them to concentrate on what they should, namely conserving their energies and feeding heavily in preparation for winter. Thus it is critical that we have well-balanced deer herds—under the carrying capacity of the range, proper buck:doe ratios, proper age-class distribution—if they are ever to be as healthy as they're capable of being. That's what we must strive for, not the needs and desires of humans, hunters, or nonhunters!

scrape much more than was previously thought. They refreshen scrapes, they urinate on them, they wait nearby, they pick up the buck's scent and search him out. At rubs, does have been observed to smell, lick, and rub them. Woods even recorded one doe rubbing her vulva on a rub. It's clear we have a lot more to learn about rubs and scrapes; the research is continuing (see Chapter 15).

In the twelve- to twenty-four-hour period before the doe's cycling in, she will in all likelihood join up with a buck. They'll then stay together until she cycles out, breeding numerous times, perhaps fifteen or more times during her twenty-four- to thirty-six-hour estrus. Breeding times are short, lasting only fifteen to twenty seconds. In the animal kingdom it is customary for prey animals to have short breeding times, compared with predatory animals, whose breeding times are ten to twenty times longer. Clearly, the shorter breeding time has important survival value.

Once the doe cycles out, she and her suitor both lose interest, and the buck is off in search of another doe to breed. He may breed anywhere from five to fifteen does during the rut, depending on his dominance rank, the population density, age-class distribution, and ratio of bucks to does. For him, the season will last for weeks, perhaps even a couple months. For each doe, it lasts only for the forty-eight to sixty hours immediately before and during her estrus.

For several years now writers in the popular press have been touting what's called the "second rut" and even, in some cases, the "third rut." These are thought to be those periods, approximately twenty-eight days after the primary rut (and again, twenty-eight days later), when does, mostly yearling does, that have not been impregnated and cycle in late are bred. These periods are said to provide some of the hottest deer hunting action of the whole year. Writers make such statements as, "Every buck in the woods lines up to chase these does!" Like many things one reads, the facts don't support the claims.

Lambiase et al. (1972) showed that most bucks produce sperm from mid-August to March. The number of sperm per ejaculation, however, peaks in mid-November and is only half as strong by mid-December. Having chased and bred does nonstop for weeks, by late November the bucks simply lose interest; they're tired, and they want rest and food, not sex.

Former researcher turned writer John Ozoga believes in what he calls "a window of breeding activity," which varies by region. "In nature," he says, "fawns need to be born on schedule to survive. In northern climates like

Michigan, that means late May to early June. Consequently, the further north one goes, the narrower the window of breeding activity." This makes sense to me, and other researchers seem to agree, too.

During three years of recording, dating, and measuring scrapes and rubs, I found only a handful (less than 1 percent) of active scrapes after December 5, and the percentage of rubs was small, too (less than 5 percent). I've never seen a frenzied level of breeding into December in Michigan, though so many yearling does are bred then. Secondary ruts may occur in the Deep South, but in Michigan, December breeding is very low-key, mostly nocturnal, and very much a hit-and-miss proposition conducted, I believe, by the smaller, younger bucks.

During my years of field work, I kept track of the number of deer seen together (see *Table 3.1*). Clearly, after the gun season marks the beginning of a coalescence of groups in Michigan. While groups average 2.7 deer in July, they

January	5.6	July	2.7
February	6.1	August	4.0
March	6.6	September	2.3
April	1.7	October	1.8
May	1.5	November	1.4
June	2.3	December	5.2

Table 3.1 Numbers of deer seen per sighting by month

Numbers of deer seen per deer sighting (per group) increase each year beginning in early December and show continued increase until sometime in late March. This late winter/early spring decrease is very weather-dependent. As soon as winter weather breaks the deer begin their hyperactive spring phase of behaviors. Initially, while doing so, they remain in their larger winter groupings. These groups begin splintering, however, within a week to ten days of this weather-related change. Once the groups begin cleaving, further separation is both rapid and dramatic. Group sizes will go from eight to twelve deer being commonplace to one to three being commonplace in a matter of a week or so.

Groupings gradually increase, beginning in early July, until early September, when they very rapidly decrease. When poaching/hunting/rutting pressures diminish in early December, groupings quickly increase in size again.

average 5.2 in December and 6.1 in February. Biologists theorize that this is an evolutionary leftover from a time when deer were much more heavily preyed upon than they are today. There's safety in numbers—more eyes, ears, and noses to detect danger.

My own finding is contrary to that in the literature: in southern Michigan, groupings are not separated by gender. What I've observed is mixed groups, comprised, to be sure, of female family units, but with adult bucks mixed in. Very, very often I've seen one, two, or three antlered bucks in these groups, and I've never seen a bachelor group of exclusively males between October and mid-May in southern Michigan. The groups I've seen stay together, feed, bed, and travel together until winter breaks in late March, then begin to splinter as the deer vacate their wintering areas. This splintering is gradual; the groups cleave more and more as spring green-up arrives until by mid-May we've come full cycle once again to the isolating of the does, the forced independence of the yearlings, and the beginnings of a coalescence of buck groups.

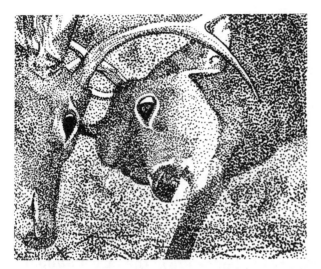

4

Deer to Deer Interactions

Whitetails are gregarious, social animals. With the possible rare exception of some lone bucks—and these may not really exist—their daily lives are spent in close association with other deer. Interactions between deer are, therefore, important to understand. The behavioral biologists who study these interactions generally break them down into three categories: aggressive acts, mutual grooming, and leadership. In reality, all of these behaviors probably represent the social expression of dominance rankings.

AGGRESSIVE ACTS

All whitetails use, clearly understand, and react to these so-called stereotypical behaviors. They are the day-to-day expressions and enforcers of dominance. Their function is to alert other deer to the intentions of the aggressor. In this way, dominance can be imposed—or challenged—by clearly defined rules.

The least aggressive act is the direct or "hard" stare. The aggressor simply stares at the other animal, generally with ears laid back along the neckline. If the animal receiving the threat is intimidated, it will look away, averting eye contact. If he/she meets and holds the stare, this shows an intention to challenge the aggressor.

The next higher level of aggression is the "head-high" and the "head-low" threat. These postures are coupled with the hard stare and clearly announce to the target animal the intention of the aggressor to make an attack, if the lesser animal does not give ground. The head-high threat, when met, is often followed by the rearing of the aggressor. He or she will then "flail" at the target animal with the front feet if ground is not given. The head-low threat is most often followed by the "chase," in which the aggressor will run the target animal off. Chasing is often culminated with a front leg kick or "leg slap," in which the aggressor quickly raises a front leg into the side or hind quarters of the target animal.

Aggressive acts of bucks and does are identical, except when the bucks have hardened antlers. Polished-antlered bucks will use antler thrusts instead of the front leg kick. In addition, they frequently use their antlers to spar and, occasionally, to fight with other bucks. In the unnatural circumstance when deer are penned, bucks have been known to kill does during rutting-related aggressive acts when, because of being penned up, they could not escape. Such behavior, as far as I know, never occurs in the wild.

Aside from rutting behavior in bucks—a special case I'll discuss separately—aggressive acts always serve the same ends and involve the same actions regardless of the sex or age of the animals involved. Aggressive acts, including those among bucks in the fall, always involve the allocation of resources. (Sexual rights represent a resource to be allocated according to dominance among whitetails.) Occasionally, a doe becomes aggressive if she perceives her fawn(s) to be threatened. Occasionally, deer become aggressive over bedding sites. But almost all nonrutting aggressive acts I've ever witnessed have arisen over food. Therefore aggression, the outward expression of dominance, is evident in all groups of deer.

The observable expression of dominance is much more common whenever resources are scarce; e.g., during winter in the far North or periods of drought in the Southwest. Accordingly, aggression is more common as the food plane decreases. If deer densities are equal, a heavily forested region will have a higher frequency of aggressive acts than an agricultural area or an area with good habitat diversity. In southern Michigan, food is so readily available most of the time that I see very few signs of aggression there, compared with what's common in the Upper Peninsula.

Mutual grooming behaviors are common and serve the critical need of strengthening the social bonds of the animals involved.

MUTUAL GROOMING

Behaviorists often speak of something called "displaced aggression." Mutual grooming (whether in the whitetail or the baboon) is a classic example. Grooming is almost always initiated by a subordinate animal and is almost always directed to a part of the body that the animal being groomed cannot reach. The head, neck, and front portions of the torso are the most common sites. It's thought that such behaviors help to strengthen social bonds within the group. From an evolutionary perspective, dominance in the group serves to assure that the fittest animals will have the greatest chance of survival; but cohesiveness of the group is equally important since there's safety in numbers for the group as a whole. Social behaviors such as grooming foster cohesiveness.

LEADERSHIP

Leadership is often thought to be a separate issue from dominance. Leadership roles change or shift continually from one animal to another. I don't agree that it's a separate issue. I believe that the shifting of leadership, like mutual grooming, is a social act that strengthens group cohesiveness.

The only animals you won't see in leadership roles are young fawns; all other animals (including yearlings) seem to take turns. In a potentially dangerous situation, the first animal to detect the danger, most often, assumes the leadership role.

DOE TO DOE INTERACTIONS

Because does and fawns form the bulk of most deer herds, the highest number of deer to deer interactions are between does. Within a family unit, dominance is not normally in question. Each member of the family knows its dominance ranking, so all it normally takes is a low-level aggressive act, e.g., a hard stare or head-high or head-low posture, to send a clear reminder. Since dominance changes over time, however, a threat can be challenged, in which case more intense levels of aggression will follow. Normally among does the most dominant animals are the oldest, biggest, and strongest.

It's among deer in aggregate groups (groups brought together by periods of diminished resources, e.g., winter yarding areas, restricted water supply) that dominance issues are most frequently and seriously challenged. This is when the true aggressive nature of the whitetail is most apparent. At these times aggression is frequent and dominance hotly contested.

DOE TO FAWN INTERACTIONS

Not infrequently you may see a doe defend her fawn(s), perhaps over the positioning of the deer. The doe gets between her fawn(s) and whatever other deer she perceives to be a threat. Then the issue is between her and the perceived aggressor, not the aggressor and the fawn(s). This type of defense is most common in yarding areas. It quickly diminishes during spring and ends entirely with the separation of the dam in late spring. From then on, the yearling is entirely on his/her own.

Outside of the case of a perceived threat to a fawn, dominance always reflects differences in size and strength. Does are invariably dominant over any fawn, regardless of the fawn's sex.

FAWN TO FAWN INTERACTIONS

Clearly, there are individual differences in the temperament of deer. Some are much more aggressive than others, and nowhere is this more evident than in the interactions between fawns. Buck fawns tend to be dominant over same-age doe fawns; however, because of their rapid growth, quickly evolving capabilities, and their innate desire to test everything, dominance issues are hotly contested among fawns. Usually the biggest are the most dominant, but this may change as an individual growth spurt kicks into overdrive and makes a particular fawn suddenly bigger.

BUCK TO BUCK INTERACTIONS

Throughout most of the year, issues of dominance between bucks are settled in exactly the same way as they are between all other deer. The same sequence of stereotypical postures and behaviors are used, with outcomes usually determined by size and strength (normally a reflection of age).

During the various phases of the rut, the most important dominance issue is at stake: breeding rights. The rut begins with the hardening of the bucks' antlers in mid-September. Sparring begins immediately thereafter and

Just as humans need not have direct, face-to-face interactions with others to exert our influence, so it is with deer. This buck, through his scent-marking behaviors, most assuredly has an impact upon every other deer that happens to discover it. Science is just beginning to unravel the secrets of precisely how.

intensifies until around mid-October, when the bucks drift apart, bachelor groups splinter and bucks become loners. Sparring involves the pushing and shoving of two or three bucks against one another, using their antlers to test their strength.

Sparring is a safe way for the bucks to work out the issue of their dominance, and it prepares them, both physically and psychologically, for the rut. It prepares a buck physically by fostering the growth and strength of the neck muscles, which may build up an additional ten inches or more before the rut begins. Psychological preparation occurs in the form of the assertiveness training that sparring provides, so the buck will learn to be sufficiently assertive sexually. By the end of the prerut sparring period, each buck knows his dominance ranking. Near-equal bucks that are unknown to each other because they have had little or no contact during the prerut phase are the ones most likely to fight each other during the rut.

True fights occur only during the "courtship" or "chase" phase of the rut and during the actual breeding phase. Then breeding is what's important, and if near-equal bucks have not settled their dominance ranking in the prolonged prerut sparring period, the dominance issue must be settled in a much more dangerous way.

Fights are ferocious, often bloody, and sometimes fatal. Vicious cuts and puncture wounds are common; eyes can be lost and antlers broken. When antlers are not "locked," fights can last anywhere from a few seconds to thirty minutes or longer. When the loser admits defeat, he'll run away if he is still able to. The victor may pursue him for a short distance, but he'll allow him to depart. Fights in which antlers are locked will usually end in the slow, pitiful death of both combatants.

Like does in aggregate groups, bucks in aggregate groups also are the most likely to engage in dominance challenges. When bucks are forming bachelor groups in the spring, for example, they often display the aggressive acts described above.

BUCK TO DOE INTERACTIONS

It's almost always implied—and frequently explicitly stated—that bucks are always dominant over does. That is simply not true. A mature, physically fit buck is dominant over other deer as long as he is the biggest, strongest deer in the area. But let that buck expend huge sums of energy during the rut, losing his weight and strength advantage, and he may well go into the crucial winter period in a subdominant position in which other bucks in better shape and some of the mature does will dominate him. Mature dominant bucks can lose as much as 20 percent to 25 percent of their body weight during the rut.

Smaller, less dominant bucks will be dominated by mature does at all times of year, including all phases of the rut. Dominance is determined by size, strength, and aggressiveness, not by gender.

5

Deer Interactions with Other Animals

I'm certain there is more to learn about deer to deer interactions, even though they seem pretty straightforward; however, interactions between deer and other species of animals are far more difficult to comprehend. Most are unpredictable, some are comical, and some are totally incomprehensible. I can tell you they are almost always entertaining.

I remember a morning in mid-November many years ago when I was sitting beside Michigan's Au Sable River. All of a sudden a little fork-horn buck came running flat out, up a small ravine I was watching. I was puzzled as to what had spooked him. I was certain no one was in the immediate area other than myself, and I knew I hadn't jumped him. As I watched him run up the ravine, I heard a noise beside me. When I glanced over, I saw a big, beautiful red fox hot on the trail of the buck. He was probably a hundred yards or so behind the buck, but he was clearly chasing him. Why would the buck run from the fox? The fox was not a physical threat to the deer. Had the deer been recently pursued by coyotes and was a little jumpy as a result? Were they simply playing with each other? It would be interesting to have answers to these questions.

Most frequently it has been fawns I've seen interacting with other animals. I don't mean to minimize the complexity of such interactions, but it sure is easy to believe one is simply witnessing the rambunctiousness of youth.

While Annette and I were taking our evening drive a couple of years ago, we were watching a group of six or seven does and fawns when I noticed something running out beyond the deer. Training my spotting scope in that direction, I saw two half-grown raccoons running along the edge between a swamp and a freshly cut wheat field. All of a sudden one of the fawns took off after the raccoons. Quickly closing the gap to ten or fifteen feet, the fawn began bouncing, thudding its front feet hard into the ground.

One raccoon stopped; the other began backing up in typical raccoon fashion with its back all hunched up. When the fawn passed the first raccoon and had its back to it, that coon charged after it. The second coon backed up until it was against a thick stand of cattails and just stood its ground. It seemed clear the fawn was having a great time. It would jump at the coons, then jump quickly away. It would run in tight little circles, then dash back at the coons.

I am familiar enough with the aggressive posturing of raccoons to know that this encounter was no fun for them. They were clearly feeling threatened by this crazed little deer running at them. But for a good four or five minutes, the fawn played until, probably winded, it slowed down. It walked very stiff-legged up to one of the coons, then leaned forward to smell it. At that point the coon swatted at the fawn with a front foot. I was too far away to see if he connected or not, but the fawn had had enough and ran back to the other deer.

Meanwhile the other deer totally ignored the commotion except for one doe—probably the fawn's dam—who raised her head for a moment to see what was going on before going back to her feeding. Adults, she seemed to say, don't have time for such silliness.

Are such encounters a form of idle silliness? Or are they a way for young deer to learn about the world around them? I strongly believe that it is the latter. True, the fawn's playful behavior, if directed toward a dangerous animal like a coyote, a bear, or a poisonous snake, could get the fawn killed. But I believe these encounters represent important learning experiences. From the perspective of the deer herd as a whole, if a fawn is lost through a foolish encounter because of inexperience, that is still better than the loss of an adult, who would have consumed far more resources of the herd. To the whitetail community, the adult is of greater survival value than is the fawn. (Besides, although I have not observed it directly, I like to think the fawn's dam or some other experienced deer would intervene if the encounter were life threatening.)

The resources the animal community invests in a member are not just those of food and water, but also the experience and knowledge of its members.

In early June 1991, I saw a fox running along the border between a fallow field and a mowed field. In both fields there were widely scattered apple trees. In a few seconds, a doe came running along, hot on the heels of the fox. When the doe got to the point where the fox had jumped into the taller weeds of the fallow field, she stopped. She stood there for several seconds, staring intently into the field, then she turned and quickly went to the base of an apple tree. After ten or fifteen seconds she left, going back in the direction she'd come from (downwind).

I was curious. After she left, I went out to the apple tree. Sure enough, there lay a newborn fawn. How much leeway does a dam allow? How often is potential danger checked out? How many predators are run off in the course of a fawn's safe growth and development? A brash, playful encounter of youth may result in a fatal encounter—or an adult with more experience, knowledge, and survival capability, and that is what's important for the well-being of the herd.

When I began research for this book, one of the things I wanted to study was whether activity levels in deer could be predicted by observing the activity levels of other animals. Specifically, if other animals are active on a given day (or during a given time period), will deer be active then, too? For comparison I chose song and game birds, squirrels and rabbits. My results? With the exception of one weather-related factor, I found no correlation.

If weather has been uncomfortable for at least ten or twelve hours, compared with the weather preceding that period, then as soon as the weather moderates, *all* animals seem to become more active.

With that exception, I saw no correlation between the various species I observed. Many days when the deer were active I saw very few other animals. Other days, when the squirrels or rabbits were active, I saw few deer. Birds always seem to be active, especially song birds in winter.

Squirrels (as well as other animals) are extremely active and noisy. They'll often make a ruckus over seemingly insignificant things, but this is done to alert others of their species that they're there, still occupying *their* territory. Such behavior is rarely designed to alert members of other species. I watched this bedded doe and feeding squirrel for well over an hour; they paid little attention to one another.

Repeatedly I was struck by how rare it is for animals to show any kind of response at all to other species. In February 1992, I was watching a doe and her fawns feeding through some hardwoods. A fox squirrel was feeding there, too. On numerous occasions the squirrel was almost between the legs of the deer. Yet the squirrel didn't react to them, nor they to it.

In December 1993, I was watching a small buck as he lay chewing his cud. A partridge came along and fed within five feet of the buck. He would occasionally watch the bird, but other than that, each essentially ignored the other. Within fifteen minutes the bird fed out of my sight while the buck continued chewing his cud.

Do you ever wonder what's the matter with the other animals where you hunt deer? I do! In most deer hunting stories I read, every animal around knows when a deer is coming. The squirrels chatter, and the blue jays yell an alert, "Wake up! Here they come!" The animals where I hunt—and I hunt a lot of different places—must be drugged! They let the deer walk all over the place without so much as a peep. It's really aggravating. If I had all those informers working for me, the way they apparently work for every other outdoor writer, I'd be a lot more successful than I am.

Seriously, I've never noticed animals react much to those of other species. Why should they? With the exception of direct competitors for food or those in a predator/prey relationship, there's no reason for animals to react to other species. Every species has its own agenda, so to speak. They have their own times to feed, to breed, to be active, to rest, and so on. Other cohabitants of the area are of little importance to them. In my experience, even competitors interact with each other minimally; they do not go through life chattering at one another. Blue jays and squirrels, it seems to me, have better things to do with their time than to worry about what the deer are doing, and (except for occasional playful encounters) the same is true for the deer.

Section II

Stresses in the Life of the Deer

The demands that life places on animals, man included, vary constantly throughout the animals' life cycle. Stress varies by season; it varies with climatic change; it varies with illness, disease, or injury; it varies because of psychological turmoil; and it varies with age. There are so many stressors no one can list them all or rank them or know precisely the energy cost of each. But we can discuss the typical stressors in the whitetail's life.

GROWTH AND DEVELOPMENT DEMANDS

In life, timing is everything, and nowhere is that more evident than in the struggles of the white-tailed deer in the far North.

There is no other time of year when so much is available with such high nutritive value for so long a period with such a merciful climate as in early June. If Mother Nature is true to form, days are warm but not oppressively hot. The threat of cold, wet weather is minimal. Water is readily available, and even when it rains, it's generally warm rain.

Vegetative growth is rapid, abundant, and more nutritious (higher protein level) than at any other time of the year.

Biologists speak of a "window of opportunity" for the survival of fawns. The first two weeks of June is that window period in the far North. The farther south you go, the wider the window gets, but there are dangers and constraints in the South. They are simply different constraints and in some ways less predictable. An example is the higher incidence of disease found in the South. As grim and punishing as winter can be in the North, the cold has an advantage—it kills off the microbes that bring disease.

Spreading out the birthing period over time in the South is an evolutionary insurance policy against losing the entire fawn crop in the event of unusual climatic hardship or its aftereffects.

In the North, if fawns are not born when they "should" be, they simply won't survive. There will be neither resources nor time for all the necessary growth and development tasks that must be accomplished before winter's icy grip.

Lactation is physiologically demanding on a doe. This is especially true when the doe is an immature animal herself (if she's a yearling with a fawn). If sufficient resources are not readily available to her—quality foodstuffs and sufficient moisture—neither she nor the fawn may survive.

The fawn's body demands huge quantities of energy per pound—more than at any other time in the deer's life—for growth and development. The doe's milk is richer in fat, protein, dry solids, and energy than cow's milk (Silver 1961). During the first thirty days of life fawns gain an average of .44 pounds per day, tripling their weight gain in the first month (Verme 1961).

How quickly and how much a fawn turns to forage depends on how much milk the dam produces and on whether the fawn is single or one of twins or triplets. The less the milk supply for any reason, the earlier and more heavily the deer will turn to forage.

Within three or four weeks all fawns will generally be foraging, and by four or five weeks they should be obtaining roughly 50 percent of their caloric intake by foraging. At roughly two months of age (first of August) they will be functioning ruminants and, if not totally weaned, nursing seldom. Some does are more indulgent than others, letting fawns nurse for another month or even six weeks. I have never taken a "northern" doe during the various hunting seasons I've participated in that was still nursing, but in December 1994 I hunted in south Texas and did take one there.

At this point and lasting until late autumn, fawns need high-quality forage. They must again nearly double their body weight between early August and November, if they are to have a good chance of surviving the winter. As mentioned in Chapter 1, if deer densities are equal, survival is more difficult for forest-land whitetails than for those living in diversified or agricultural habitats, where the nutritional plane is always higher. In the North, fawns need to enter winter weighing at least fifty-five to sixty pounds to have a realistic chance of survival.

DEMANDS OF THE RUT

Nature has a way of balancing the physiological stresses between the sexes. Pregnancy, lactation, and mothering are all very draining for does. The male segment of the herd has its highest energy drain during the rut.

Predation research on wolves, mountain lions, and (to a much lesser extent) coyotes shows that it is the young, the old, the ill, the injured, and the male segments of the deer population that are the most vulnerable to predation. (Bucks also perish from nonpredatory, natural causes at a higher rate than does during the winter period.) The reason for this is the emaciated condition of many bucks, especially prime-age dominant bucks, resulting from the two-month period of intense, nonstop expenditure of energy during the rut. As mentioned in Chapter 2, a buck can lose up to 25 percent of his body weight between the first of October and early December.

Although not evident in the photo, this buck was demonstrating the typical rigors of the rut for a dominant animal when I photographed him. His sides were heaving, his mouth was agape, and he was wild with frustration and/or anger. Such unrelenting forces literally compel dominant bucks to expend huge sums of energy for weeks, often sealing their fate when winter arrives.

Beginning in mid-September bucks increase their energy expenditure while decreasing their energy intake. This is most dramatic among prime-age dominant bucks. In mid-September bucks are in the best condition they'll enjoy until the following late spring. They weigh more, have greater fat reserves, have more energy, and are more physically fit than at any other time. A prime-age buck is the very essence of power, elegance, beauty, alertness, and enthusiasm, but by early December the same buck will often be gaunt, weak, exhausted, and injured. It's not because of food shortage. It's because for those two months a buck has only one objective besides surviving: breeding.

Many writers suggest that bucks become incredibly reckless at this time. That is not true. Bucks not experienced in the ways of hunters may unwittingly expose themselves to danger, but bucks accustomed to hunters are sharply alert. If they don't survive long enough to breed, they can't pass on their genes, which is the biological imperative, the driving force, behind everything they do. In the process they may become so totally spent that they succumb to winter's ravages, but that is a price nature allows them to risk only after breeding is accomplished. From the perspective of the herd—the only perspective that matters—the buck's loss after breeding is unfortunate but tolerable.

As September slides into October, sparring, rubbing, and scraping increase. Feeding decreases, gradually at first, then more quickly as time passes. By mid-October, the chase phase of the rut has begun, and it increases in intensity for the next few weeks. Sparring decreases (for the bigger bucks), rubbing and scraping increase, and fights become more common. Chasing and testing doe after doe for her receptiveness create a huge energy drain.

Feeding declines dramatically now, until early December. Younger bucks, not as involved in the rut, continue to feed but at a reduced level. The older buck stops eating not by conscious decision; hormones undoubtedly make the decision for him.

In early November, as the first does cycle in, the buck breeds and this serves only to heighten his interest and desire. Feeding stops entirely as he begins really chasing the does. He's frustrated; he rubs violently, destroying any bush or small tree that lies in his path. He scrapes and checks them often, hoping to find another receptive doe, but at this point they're few and far between. Finally, toward the latter part of November, after nearly two weeks of nonstop, frantic activity, all the does begin cycling in.

Now the buck finds does everywhere that are willing and receptive. He'll spend a day or two with each, breeding repeatedly. After ten days of this, he's physically spent and

It's critical that all the deer in a herd and their state of breeding readiness be synchronized. We've not unraveled all the mysteries of how this is accomplished, but it's evident that all the sign we see and all the activities we've recorded play a role in it. This is a fairly typical, late-prebreeding buck rub.

needs rest. As the last of the does cycle out, his desire diminishes and his thoughts turn to food. With winter closing in, is he too far gone to recover? Only Mother Nature will decide. Either way, he's fulfilled his biological role. Incidentally, this all-out expenditure of energy for breeding is not unique to whitetails; it's quite common among many other vertebrate species too.

PREGNANCY

The doe, in the meantime, has been feeding steadily all autumn. She's heavier now than at any other time of year. She's pregnant and in great shape. Occurring as it does in the winter months, when food is scarce and weather merciless, pregnancy obviously represents a tremendous physiological stress; however, nature minimizes the stress by staggering embryo and fetal development in a way that optimizes the chances for survival of both doe and fawn.

From the moment of conception (roughly November 23 in southern Michigan) studies show there is a period of thirty days before implantation occurs (Robinette et al. 1955). This delay in implantation means that the embryonic

The doe in autumn is at her physical optimum. She's heavier now than at any other time and, except for a three- or four-day period for each doe, is little affected by the activities of the rut. Nature, as it always seems to do, has devised a system to balance the demands placed upon the sexes. All the incessant activities of the bucks are geared toward the impending pregnancy of the does. From the perspective of the herd, the buck's demise following breeding is tolerable as long as the doe's fertilization is assured.

blastoderm requires absolutely no energy input from the doe for a month. All the energy required during this time is supplied by the yolk within the fertilized ovum.

After implantation, the blastoderm becomes a blasto-cyst and then, some fifteen days later, an embryo. Now there is rapid cellular differentiation (specialization of tis-sue types) and placental development, and this growth spurt begins to tax the doe. The growth spurt begins abrupt-ly around the end of December, and energy demands on the doe increase rapidly over the next month. By mid-February the embryo has formed all of the necessary tissue types, has a long axis and all of its major structures. It now weighs roughly ten to twelve ounces and is considered a fetus.

A quiescent period now begins, how quiescent depend-ing on the doe's nutritional status. If she's well-fed, it's not as dramatic, and fetal development will continue, although at a slower rate. If she's already catabolizing her fat reserves and carrying one fawn, growth can stop almost completely. If she's carrying twins, a phenomenon known as physical dimorphism often occurs, in which one twin ceases to grow while the other continues to grow, but at a much reduced rate. If the dam is severely malnourished, she'll abort her fawn(s).

The quiescent period lasts until spring green-up or very shortly before, when the doe's metabolic rate (the rate at which she burns energy) increases. The more severe the nutritional shortage or the longer it lasts, the more pro-found the effect on both doe and fawn(s). Danger arises now because photoperiodism controls the deer's metabolic rate, whereas weather controls spring green-up. The metabolic rate *will* increase on schedule; spring green-up *may*.

Natal mortality, even adult mortality, will run exceed-ingly high during severe winters, especially if followed by a late spring. Does that lose their fawns recover more quickly and have a better chance of success with subsequent preg-nancies than does that have viable births but are severely taxed by them.

A tremendous growth spurt that drives the fetus to at least triple its weight begins with normal spring green-up (mid-April in southern Michigan) and ends with the birth of the fawn(s) six or seven weeks later. This is the phase of greatest weight gain for the fetus, and success or failure very much depends on the availability of new vegetative growth at this time.

LACTATION AND MOTHERING

The strain of lactation on the doe is part of the price she must pay for her successful pregnancy. The physical and psychological demands of mothering require additional energy. The cost of these energy drains will be paid not now, but rather in her preparedness for the following year. If she was malnourished enough so her reserves were at a bare minimum when she delivered, she may not have time enough to recoup her losses by autumn, and next year's pregnancy will more likely end in abortion, a prenatal death, or her own death!

Lactation is demanding at least until early August, with the average doe producing between thirty to fifty ounces of milk per day during peak nursing. Milk production depends on age (first-time dams usually produce less milk), on whether she's born single or multiple fawns, and on her nutritional status. Research shows that the quality of a dam's milk is not reduced, although quantity is, if she's malnourished. In southern Michigan such malnourishment is practically unheard of (unless the dam is injured or diseased), but it is not uncommon in the North.

I've never read about the demands of mothering fawns, but it would be a serious mistake to underestimate them. Just ask a human mother what is the most difficult part of a mother's role. I'm willing to bet she won't say pregnancy or nursing, but rather all the years of caring for the kids! When I asked my wife, Annette, how much time she spent thinking about and watching the kids, her response was immediate: "Twenty-four hours a day!"

Remember the doe I saw checking on her fawn after the fox went by (Chapter 5)? How many such instances of vigilance does the average doe put into successfully rearing a fawn? No one knows, of course, but such vigilance represents a significant strain on every dam.

ANTLER DEVELOPMENT

There's a slight energy demand on a mature buck from toting around three to six pounds of antler mass in winter, but the bulk of the physiological expense is during the growing phase each year between mid-April and mid-September. Some theorists have suggested that the energy demand of antler growth is equal to that of pregnancy. I don't think so. At least two major differences negate that comparison. First, energy expended for antler growth is diverted for that purpose only after the bodily nutritional needs of the buck have been met. Second, the antler growth period coincides with the time of greatest nutritional opulence and of minimum weather-related stress.

Antlers are made of bone. They differ from other bone in that they are solid; i.e., they have no lumen and, therefore, produce no marrow. They consist of a framework (matrix) of mineralized (ossified) cells. Eighty-five to 90 percent of their mass is made up of calcium and phosphorous.

Antler growth among various members of the deer family (Cervidae) is truly phenomenal. It is the only known mammalian structure ever regenerated and the fastest growing bone known to science. In fact, the only faster growing mammalian tissue known is that of some forms of cancer. The annual growth of the whitetails' antlers is amazing enough, but that of other North American members of the family is simply astounding: moose, elk, caribou, and mule deer. Of all the family members, caribou (pictured here) typically grow larger antlers per unit of body mass than any other deer, and they do so in approximately a five-month growing season each year, starting from scratch.

They're attached to the buck's skull by growth plates called pedicles. Antlers are shed annually, while the pedicles are retained. Pedicles increase in size annually (mostly in diameter, after the first eighteen months of a buck's life). During their growth phase antlers are nourished by the highly vascular skin that covers them, called "velvet."

We often speak of antlers "hardening," by which we mean the buck is stripping the velvet from them. But antlers are calcified bone, so they actually harden as they grow. Ossification occurs as minerals move down the osmotic gradient to become embedded in the underlying protein matrix. As the minerals are deposited, the fluids that transported them are forced outward, so hardening is simply an event of growth.

Antlers grow simultaneously at the distal ends of each point and in diameter along their total length. Growth slows, then ceases as testosterone levels increase in late summer. Blood supply to the antlers diminishes over a two-week period as testosterone levels rise. The so-called "burrs" (bumpy ridges at the antlers' base) increase in size and actually strangulate the blood vessels until blood flow stops. Then, it's believed, the shrinking velvet may "itch" the buck, causing him to rub the velvet off. Some bucks, however, lose their velvet without rubbing; it simply shrivels when deprived of blood and, like dry skin, flakes off.

ILLNESS AND DISEASE

Illness is defined as any significant deviation from "normal," while disease is a profound and (if identified) predictable course of symptoms that can affect all or part of the body. Etiology, pathology, and prognosis of a disease may be known or unknown. Illness and disease are very common among deer, but somewhat less common in the northern portions of the whitetails' range. The reason they're more common in the South is because of the way in which diseases are spread among creatures living in the wild. The major carriers of disease—mosquitoes, flies, gnats, ticks, snails—either die out annually or become otherwise isolated in the North. In addition, a deer that is severely weakened by illness or disease is more likely to succumb to the process in the North, and is thereby less likely to transmit the disease to others. In the North, most illnesses and diseases claim their victims during winter; in the South, it's more likely during extreme heat or drought. Following is a partial list of the most common diseases among deer.

Epizootic Hemorrhagic Disease (EHD). A highly fatal disease that kills by extensive hemorrhaging of various internal organs. The disease has a very sudden onset, usually in late summer or early autumn. Whitetails are particularly susceptible, but mule deer and pronghorn antelope have suffered losses, too. I know of only one confirmed outbreak in Michigan, but it can occur anywhere, most commonly in the South and West.

Anthrax. An acute (rapid onset and progression) infectious disease caused by *Bacillus anthracis*, an organism found worldwide. Transmission occurs in several ways, generally by soil or water contamination. It is a highly contagious disease, to which humans are also very susceptible. Infected animals usually die within forty-eight hours.

Foot rot. Most common during dry weather in late summer/early autumn and spread by direct contact with contaminated soil, usually around watering holes. Fawns are most susceptible. Affects feet and mouth, both of which develop ulcerations. The animal runs a high fever, stops feeding, and salivates excessively. Infected animals may recover. Very widespread.

Tuberculosis. Since 1980, tuberculosis is on the rise, after decades of decline, among humans. Since whitetails are known carriers and may live in proximity to humans, they need to be monitored closely, although they rarely show actual symptoms of the disease.

Actinomycosis. A widespread infectious disease, also called "lumpy jaw." Caused by an organism common in poor-quality feed, particularly hay. Infection is usually in the mandible (jaw), and the bone is destroyed. Common in aged and artificially fed deer. Not normally fatal.

Salmonellosis. A bacterial disease spread by ingestion of contaminated soil or feed. Common in newborns, pretty much limited to the South. Always fatal.

It is not my intent to detail all of the illnesses and diseases among the whitetail, but only to highlight the most common. The reader should know that illness and disease, even when they do not kill outright, may be very taxing and leave a deer weakened so that it is less able to survive some challenge later on. Two examples of this follow. The direct quotes are from *White-Tailed Deer: Ecology and Management*, a Wildlife Management Institute book (Kingston 1981).

Theileriosis. Spread by ticks, this disease is common in our southwestern states. "In Texas more than 57 percent of the white-tailed deer carry the parasite. Infectious rates are highest when deer density is high and nutritional level low. Clinical disease and mortality usually occur in deer that have experienced environmental stress, such as may be caused by severe weather and food shortages."

Sarcocystis. A protozoan organism found in striated muscles of many wild creatures. "Most adult deer are infested with sarcocytes, but alone the sarcocytes do not cause overt sign of illness."

When you add the physiological stress of illness or disease to the stresses of the life cycle and those ever-present in the environment, it is clear that any one of these may be the straw that finally does the camel in—or in this case, the deer. This is why it is so important that we maintain optimum habitats and contain deer herds within the constraints of their range in order to minimize the stresses as much as we can.

SENESCENCE

I have devoted more than fifteen years of my professional life to the care of elderly humans in geriatric settings. I love older people. I admire their gentle determination, their soft demeanor, the wisdom and insight gained through their life experiences. They truly seem to have a better perspective on dealing with life. I resent bitterly what time has done to them and strive to do what I can to make them happy, comfortable, and fulfilled. Heart disease, osteoporosis, circulatory insufficiency, vision failure, hearing loss, and so on. Add to these loneliness, isolation, and loss of loved ones—life can be very tough for some people!

It's much the same for the whitetail. Autopsies of older deer repeatedly show a wide variety of organ-system failures (senescence), and an accumulation of assorted injuries. When the deer of Michigan and other cold climes go into the winter months already burdened with assorted maladies, their chances of survival are greatly reduced. Even if they're lucky enough to survive this year, they probably won't the next.

The Observation and Study of Deer

Just about the strangest experience I ever had with a deer occurred during the first spring of my field study for this book. June 5, 1991, was a typical late spring day: sunny, about seventy degrees, with moderately gusty winds. I was walking on a well-used runway through a fallow field with pockets of brush interspersed with patches of high, dense weeds. I was looking for deer sign more than deer, and I was walking downwind. All of a sudden I heard a commotion about twenty yards in front of me. I looked up to see a deer burst forth out of a patch of grassy weeds and head in my direction. There happened to be a thick bush right beside me, and I quickly took a step behind it. The bush was short, and I towered over it by at least two feet. Other than taking the one step, I'd made little movement and less noise. The deer kept coming directly at me. In that split moment, all I could think was, "That deer's attacking me!"

That in itself is funny, because I'm probably the least likely person to believe such a thing. But I thought I must have gotten between a doe and her fawn and that the doe was coming after me. The deer continued down the run, passing me at a distance of one foot. As it ran past I saw it was not a doe but a young buck with small spikes, two or three inches long. He ran ten or fifteen feet beyond me and stopped. He threw his head around in a clear attempt to discover what had disturbed him. I stood frozen.

The young buck's gaze kept going back and forth between the thicket he'd been in and the upwind side of the thicket. It felt like he stared right at me several times but did not see me. Within half a minute he began to relax. His ears shifted, his muscles relaxed, and his gaze became less intense as he swished his tail back and forth a couple times. His body language suggested he was confused. He seemed to be thinking, "I could swear I smelled something." But by then, despite the swirling gusts, he was clearly upwind of me and couldn't smell me. After another few seconds, he walked away. I watched until he disappeared into a fenceline.

Along with millions of other people, I find the observation of wildlife fun and exciting, both relaxing and enjoyable. I want to share with you some simple secrets that I hope will make it better—more illuminating and educational—for you.

As a young man I had the extremely good fortune to be surrounded by some unusually brilliant professors and physicians. I admired these people tremendously and wanted to emulate them. One day, while assisting a surgical procedure, I said to the surgeon that I didn't see how I could ever expect to be in his shoes, to learn as much as he knew. He replied, "I don't really know all that much. In fact, I get frustrated at how little I know. I just know what questions to ask. That's the secret."

In the years since, I've proved over and over the wisdom of that surgeon's remarks. Asking the right questions truly is the key to getting more knowledge and more enjoyment out of whatever you do. Observing wildlife is no exception. I'm not in any way suggesting that you take a relaxing and enjoyable activity and turn it into pedantic drudgery, only that you heighten your enjoyment through deeper understanding. Questions serve to stimulate one's thought processes. Without the questions, you can make the same observations countless times, and they will have little or no meaning for you because you won't understand the behaviors behind them.

What was that young buck I jumped doing? Why did he run right at me? Could he have been attacking me? After he walked away, I went over to the thicket he'd come out of. The ground in that area was gently undulating, and the thick patch he'd been bedded in had a swirled pattern in it. Clearly, the wind usually swirled in a counterclockwise direction through that patch, and he'd detected my scent moving from his right to his left. He'd jumped and run downwind of my scent stream. When he hit the runway, he'd turned to go crosswind, but the rolling ground and swirling wind caused him to run right to me. He wasn't attacking me; he never even knew where I was.

Too often, people fail to ask the necessary questions so that they can analyze the available facts and come to the right conclusions. Without the questions, experiences like

It is hard to imagine how anyone can take wildlife for granted. Even casual, cursory observations of wildlife are much more enjoyable for those who ask questions about their observations.

mine with the young buck can lead people to believe they have been attacked—or some other incorrect belief about deer behavior.

Even if your interest lies only in the casual observation and enjoyment of the outdoors, you will enjoy it more by truly thinking about what you see. That involves an active process, in which questions are the most important part. If your interests are more serious, that is, if you really want to learn more about deer and their behaviors, then some specific questions are necessary.

My first step in researching this book was to make a list of deer behaviors I often read about that simply do not agree with my own observations. I was also interested in those deer behaviors that I see but have never read about. I spent close to six months formulating questions I wanted to answer. Then I went into the field every day for three years looking for answers. I read and reread my questions. Sometimes I rewrote the questions when I realized they weren't the right ones or weren't specific enough to produce satisfactory answers. Here's a sample of the questions I asked.

How are deer distributed on a seasonal basis? Are they in the same places in summer as in winter? Are they in the same place this winter as they were last winter? How does their use of the habitat change with the seasons? In a given area do the deer do the same things they did at a different time of year? When are the deer most active on an annual, seasonal, and daily basis? Sometimes deer use primarily the "edges" of the habitat; do they always do so? Where do deer bed? Do deer feed more heavily (hence move around more) just before a storm front? Just after? Both?

Such questions serve to focus attention; without them as a guideline, it's difficult to compare what you see today with what you saw yesterday or last year. You don't have to formulate questions as specific as mine; they should be whatever questions you want answers to. I assure you questions will help you think about what it is you're seeing.

Another important habit to cultivate is to record what you've seen daily, in detail. If you're serious about observation, recording is crucial. Our memories are faulty. If we don't record, we forget details. In recording rubs each fall, for example, I carried with me a list of questions written on a three-inch by five-inch card about each rub:

>Type of tree?
>Type of cover?
>On or near runway?
>Height off the ground?
>Length of rub?
>Girth of tree?
>Extent of damage?
>Percent of girth rubbed?
>Percent of rub, if any, down to sapwood?

Sometimes there'd be as many as fifteen rubs in a small area. I dutifully measured and recorded each. But I found that if I came back to the area a week later, I couldn't remember, "Is that a new rub? Were there eleven rubs here or twelve?" I found I had to add another question to my list: How many rubs in the immediate area? But that still didn't solve the problem, because if I'd recorded, say, eleven rubs the first time, but found thirteen on a later visit, I didn't know which eleven were the original ones and which two were the new ones. Finally, I began carrying a bottle of black paint. After I recorded my findings, I'd paint a slash at the base of the tree. That way I didn't have to rely on my imperfect memory.

One more thing. Casual observation is fine; just going out to see and enjoy deer any time is great fun. But to study the deer, to begin to really understand their behavior, requires much more. The more you get out, the more you make it a habit, the more you'll learn. Hours and hours afield, though, is not necessarily the answer, because if you get bored or feel pressured that there are other things you should be doing, you won't learn as much. One or two hours a day is often enough, provided you put in enough days.

I said I was in the field every day for three years while researching this book, but that's not actually true. Some days were taken up entirely with commitments of work and family life. I took vacations. But I discovered that if I was gone for even a few days, it would take me three or four days on my return to catch up. Invariably, it seemed, in my absence the deer had begun to do something a little differently, and it took time to understand the changes. Because of all the distractions and obligations, I found I had to make field study my number one priority. I think you will find that getting out once or twice a week is just not enough if you really want to understand an animal as complex as the white-tailed deer.

Deer Herd Composition: What's Natural?

In today's world practically all deer herds are managed. What is considered a normal deer herd composition is very much dependent on the philosophy of the given manager. Nonetheless (or, perhaps, for that very reason) I think it's important to give some serious thought to what would be natural. That is, how many bucks, does, and fawns, and what age-class distribution would there be in a herd that was not managed by modern man.

We'll never know precisely the composition of pre-European deer herds. Most certainly, there could not have been a single composition standard for all herds because habitats, latitudes, and predatory factors would have caused variation. But still we can make some educated "guesstimates" about the parameters of "natural."

First of all, slightly more bucks are born than does (the ratio is 105:100), but the mortality rate is somewhat higher for buck fawns than for doe fawns, so by recruitment age (four to five months), the ratio of males to females is pretty well balanced, roughly 100:100.

Most indigenous North Americans hunted the whitetail extensively. The antlers were of symbolic importance to many of them, but the more utilitarian needs for meat, hide, sinew, and suet probably resulted in their killing without much regard for the gender of the deer. I believe it's safe to assume they probably took deer in approximately a 1:1 sex ratio, or whatever the sex ratio was of the herd in question. This was probably not the case with regard to age class; younger deer would have been taken more often, while older deer would have learned to avoid early man just as experienced deer today avoid hunters.

Historically, predators played a major role in limiting deer numbers—or at least a much greater role than they do today. Mountain lions were widespread over most of North America's whitetail range. Wolves were even more widespread than lions. Coyotes were widespread, too, but because of their predation by the lions and wolves, their numbers would have been significantly checked. The same is true for bobcat and lynx. Black bears were very common throughout all the forested regions. The grizzly was common throughout the Plains region and the entire West.

To gauge the effect of the big predators, mountain lions and wolves, we depend on the research of Hornacker et al. and Mech et al. Even with low deer densities in most areas and relatively high cat populations, the presence of other prey species served to buffer the cats' effect on deer. It seems likely that, as they do today, lions would have preyed most heavily on fawns in early summer and weakened animals in winter (deer made more vulnerable by weather, age, infirmity, or rut exhaustion).

Possibly there were regions of the country where the ratio of lions to deer exceeded the ratio Hornacker felt critical (1 lion per 135 deer) so that deer herds were limited by lions. To speculate on the composition of such a herd, it seems logical to suppose it contained relatively small recruitment cohorts and stable cohorts of 1½-, 2½-, 3½-, and 4½-year-olds of both sexes, but fairly rapid depletion of older age classes, especially older bucks. Wolves prey on basically the same age classes and individuals as lions do (Mech et al.) Among bucks, it is the older that are taken by

Mature bucks, those with such autumn elegance and beauty as this one, are quite different physically and metabolically by the end of the rut period. They're more vulnerable to winter predation than are does and fawns, because of their physical condition then and because of behavioral differences.

predators for any of the following reasons: they enter winter in a weakened condition after the rut; they frequently suffer from arthritic hind leg joints; they tend, more than does, to live on the fringes of yarding areas, where they're more vulnerable to predation.

Part-time deer predators (coyotes, bobcats, lynx, and bears) undoubtedly took fawns and the occasional adult, but then as now, they'd have been mostly carrion eaters.

Wild population fluctuations of both predators and prey seem likely. We know that both natural and man-made fires ravaged many areas repeatedly. Tornadoes and wind storms would have opened the forest canopy, too. These events would have fostered a rapid emergence of high-value foodstuffs for deer, and their population would have flourished. Of course, populations of the predators would have flourished, too, but with a time lag of one or two years. As predatory populations grew, they'd have pressured the deer and reduced their numbers. The predators' population would then crash about six months later. Periods of weather severity or moderation would repeatedly usher in cycles like this in both populations.

If reality was anything like my supposings, it seems evident that in most areas at most time periods the herds would have had a much older age structure than is usual today. Periods of rapid population growth would see a younger herd for a while, of course.

Today, deer herds in southern Michigan, and many other locales, are believed to have essentially the following compositions. Out of every hundred animals, there are forty fawns; forty does, of which fifteen are yearlings, ten are 2½-year-olds, eight are 3½-year-olds, five are 4½-year-olds, and only two are older; and twenty antlered bucks, of which fifteen are yearlings, three are 2½-year-olds, and only two are 3½-year-olds or older.

Are such musings and speculations simply an idle intellectual exercise? I don't think so. Our deer herds evolved under the competing influences of predators, weather-related stressors, and indigenous hunters for eons. Modern man has changed everything. We've eliminated most predators; we've drastically altered the habitat; we've instituted intense pressures on the male component of most modern herds; and we've radically lowered the age-group characteristics of today's herds. We've created in the past hundred years a deer society unlike any that's ever existed before. No one knows what effect these changes will have over time, but I believe we have an obligation to try to find out.

Research clearly shows that mature bucks behave differently from immature bucks. What will be the long-range effects of a relative absence of mature bucks? What are the effects of this change on does? What are the effects of having nearly half of our herds consist of fawns? Despite what some in our game departments might say, no one knows the answers to these questions. I deeply resent the arrogance of

I took this photo on October 17. Notice how small the fawn is. The fawn's dam is only a yearling herself. This fawn would need to weigh at least fifty to sixty pounds in order to have a realistic chance of winter survival. It clearly weighed less than twenty pounds! While this can happen in any deer herd, it is far more likely to occur in those with very poor age-class structure, especially in the buck segment of the herd.

DNR administrators who insist every year on playing a game of roulette with our deer. I cannot think it's wise to attempt deer herd management without answers to these and other questions. We may already have done irreparable damage to our herds. If I could have just one wish granted, it would be for money for biological research to determine the effect of man's tampering with nature. Then we could take remedial action, if it's not too late.

I'm not for an instant suggesting we stop hunting (the reality is that modern hunting, through license sales, is the fuel needed to monitor and manage *all* wildlife). I'm not even suggesting hunting be reduced—unhunted deer in excess of the habitat's carrying capacity would perish anyway, from old age, starvation, injury, disease, vehicle accidents, destroyed habitat, and so on. But I believe research would show that the composition of today's deer herds puts them in danger, danger that may be averted through human efforts. As I'll show in the next chapter, there is a sensible, easily instituted remedy, one which creates very nearly the same conditions under which the whitetail evolved.

9

Philosophies of Deer Management

Most people think that management of resources, the whitetail included, should be based on scientific fact—or at the very least, scientifically justified principles. Far too often, it is not. Economics and perceived social values, real or imagined, are the driving forces behind most management decisions. Government administrators use a variety of arguments to try to justify positions already taken. Perhaps that is human nature. But it is certainly not the wisest approach to the maintenance and protection of our wildlife.

Wildlife management became a reality in this country in 1896 in a court decision, *Geer v. Connecticut*, when the judge ruled that wild animals are owned by the state and that police powers of the state include the duty to maintain wildlife for the people. According to the Wildlife Management Institute's *White-Tailed Deer: Ecology and Management*, "a state owns the wildlife within its borders and holds it in trust for the people. And the state has an obligation to protect that trust."

It seems clear to me that a state is obligated to do its

utmost to protect its animals, both now and into the future. If economic or social considerations are put ahead of the best interest of the animals, the state is violating that trust. I'll discuss these issues with regard to my state, Michigan, but the same principles apply in any other state.

Michigan DNR administrators play a numbers game in terms of license sales and deer kill figures. Every year the DNR central office reports license sales and kill statistics prefaced by such phrases as "the best ever" or "the second highest." It reports that a certain percentage of hunters (the higher the better) were successful. It's a promotional tool for the DNR; the higher the kill this year, the greater the expectation of license sales for next year. Of course, the higher the sales, the greater their revenues. Despite their denials, their attitude clearly seems to be, "The good of the deer be damned!"

A few years ago, in an effort to spur license sales even more, the DNR went to a second license system. A hunter successfully filling his/her tag can purchase a second license and keep on hunting. DNR administrators have attempted to justify this system by saying, "Everybody does it anyway; they keep hunting until everyone within their party has filled all the tags." If that's really what hunters are doing, then where's the law enforcement division of the DNR to arrest the violators? Where are the judges needed to enforce the penalties? We can't let law violators dictate government policy! That's ridiculous!

If what the Michigan DNR is doing is wrong, then what is right? To answer that we need to focus on what it is we want to accomplish. It seems clear to me that the best management is one designed to promote the long-term survival and well-being of our deer herds. I don't think it's reasonable to ask for more than that, and I don't think it's acceptable to get any less!

Until research indicates otherwise, it seems to me only logical to try to approximate what science suggests is a natural (historic) deer herd composition, as discussed in the previous chapter. There is certainly room for legitimate dispute over what is natural or historic, but any policy not based on scientific principle is a foolish one.

The heavy preponderance of "spike" and other immature
bucks in many of today's deer herds is anything but natural!
We cannot/should not cull nearly 90 percent of our antlered
animals year after year, and then depend upon an immature buck segment of the herd to produce our offspring. It's
reckless and outrageous!

Is this possible? Is such management economically feasible? Can it be done in a state like Michigan? The answer
to all of these questions is a definite "Yes!"

Deer management practices today run the entire spec-
trum from so-called trophy management programs and
quality management to what is considered traditional deer

management (see *Illustration 9.1*). No state practices trophy management. To do so would severely restrict deer hunting opportunities and revenues and would require intense scrutiny (hence, tremendous expense). Additionally, the composition of the herd would be anything but "natural."

There are many ranches in Texas where trophy mangement has been practiced for many years now. Composition of these herds typically runs something like this: Out of every hundred deer, there are twenty fawns, thirty does, and fifty antlered bucks, of which twelve are yearlings, eleven are 2½-year-olds, nine are 3½-year-olds, and eighteen are 4½-year-olds or older. It is for these trophy animals that the herds are managed. Note the ratio of bucks to does is 2:1.

I think the performance record of these ranches speaks for itself. Despite tremendous overhead expense and a few incredible trophies, no world records have come from any of these programs—and only a few state records. The point of this discussion, however, is whether such programs are good for the deer, and I cannot see that they are. I don't see

Illustration 9.1

Trophy   Quality   Traditional
Management   Management   Management

Deer management practices and philosophies can best be viewed as lying along a continuum. Because of differing and/or fluctuating population parameters, including such things as weather, predation, hunting pressure, poaching pressure, population density, nutritional plane, the manager's or agency's stated goals, no two programs, no matter how closely monitored and regulated, can ever remain static on the line. Every program, every herd, will always be in some level of flux.

The resulting differences of importance will be: (1) buck:doe ratios; (2) population levels in relation to capacity; and (3) the age-class structure of the herd. As we move along the continuum, from left to right, these are the changes we can expect to encounter: (1) increasing population densities; (2) increasing (more skewed towards does) buck:doe ratios; and (3) decreasing age-class structure. The more natural compositions will lie within the central portions of the continuum; as we move outward, in either direction, we clearly get into less healthy situations for the deer.

anything horribly detrimental about such private management programs, since they account for such a tiny fraction of the deer population, but I'd certainly object to any state adopting such a program as public policy.

Quality management programs are in effect in several states (chiefly in the South and in some western states) and in several Canadian provinces. They are not necessarily called quality management programs, but their management philosophy promotes the same goals. Composition of these herds approximates what seems to have been the composition of natural or historic herds. Out of every hundred animals, there are twenty fawns; forty does, of which fifteen are yearlings, ten are 2½-year-olds, eight are 3½-year-olds, and seven are 4½-year-olds or older; and forty antlered bucks, of which fifteen are yearlings, ten are 2½-year-olds, eight are 3½-year-olds, and seven are 4½-year-olds or older. Note the ratio of bucks to does is 1:1.

Of course, these represent averages; real herds—whether current or historic—vary and fluctuate in composition. The key features of the optimal program are the 1:1 buck:doe ratio and containing of deer numbers under the carrying capacity of the habitat. Such a program is no more expensive to operate than a traditional management program. Recruitment rates are very high, herds are healthy, and antler growth is phenomenal. Since 1985 many state and world records have been set and reset under these programs.

Traditional deer management programs like Michigan's are in place in many states, particularly in the North, the East, and the Midwest. Typical composition in these herds is forty fawns, forty does, and twenty antlered bucks (fifteen yearlings, three 2½-year-olds, and only two 3½-year-olds or older). The ratio of bucks to does is supposed to be 1:2 under a traditional program, but in Michigan it's actually more like 1:5 or 1:10. This is anything but natural!

Needless to say, few state records are ever set under these programs, and even fewer Pope & Young or Boone & Crockett bucks are taken. What's even more disappointing from a deer hunter's perspective, all the hunting tactics and techniques one reads about that hunters in other parts of the country are having so much success and fun with cannot be used here; they simply will not work (see Chapters 15, 16, and 19).

When buck to doe ratios are so skewed that there's no competition among bucks for breeding rights, tactics such as horn rattling, calling, and the use of sexual scents are not as effective because there's no reason for the bucks to respond to them. Even buck sign is minimized in such herds, making practically any tactic ineffective. Without buck sign you cannot pattern the deer. If you cannot pattern him, buck hunting becomes a crap shoot. There's no doubt about it, Michigan hunters are getting shortchanged. More important, so are our deer!

Can Michigan turn it around? With eight hundred thousand deer hunters, could Michigan manage its herds in a quality program? You bet! Would it be economically feasible? Absolutely. If our DNR took the following nine specific steps, it could turn Michigan's program around within five years:

1. Balance the herds into approximately a 1:2 buck:doe ratio statewide
2. Reduce the overall size of the population by 10 percent to 15 percent, with most or all of the reduction in the northern lower peninsula and the western half of the Upper Peninsula
3. Eliminate second license sales
4. Eliminate landowner and block permits statewide
5. Institute a sealed licensing system, so a licensee would not know prior to buying the license whether it was a buck or doe license
6. Eliminate second archery licenses
7. Reduce the statewide buck kill by 10 percent to 15 percent annually for the first three years; then evaluate annually for adjustments
8. Put more law enforcement personnel in the field and make an effort to control poaching
9. Eliminate the traditional November 15–30 gun season and extend it instead from November 1–30 or, even better, to December 15, to eliminate the crush of humanity in the woods for the traditional two-week period

Michigan DNR administrators argue that hunting in Michigan is the way the state's hunters want it to be. They say Michigan hunters want to see twenty to fifty deer per day when they hunt, even if that means only seeing spikes—or perhaps no bucks at all.

That's ridiculous for a couple good reasons. No resource should be managed at the whim of the consumer; deer herds should be managed for the good of the deer, not the pleasure of the hunters. The DNR's argument shows circular reasoning. It has created a situation in Michigan that's far older than most of the state's deer hunters. The average Michigan deer hunter is in his mid-twenties, has never hunted anywhere but Michigan, hunts an average of three days per year, and knows little or nothing about

This poor creature is starving—we cannot justify this! For hunters to demand more deer than the habitat can support demonstrates a blatant disregard for the very animal they profess to care so much for. For the DNR to capitulate to the hunters' demands is unconscionable.

deer management principles. All he knows is what he's seen in practice here. It may be human nature to resist change, but is that a reason not to change? Of course not!

Some DNR administrators say that to change deer management policy is a societal issue. It's not. It's a problem of inertia—the DNR's. Its lethargy, lack of vision, and numbers games are leading our deer herds down a very dangerous path.

As I write this (in late January 1994), thousands of deer are starving in the western U.P. No amount of hunter satisfaction, no amount of DNR economic greed can ever justify such loss. The DNR knows very well that we're carrying way too many deer for the land to support. The state's hunters—those who cry foul whenever doe permit quotas are raised—must stand up and be accountable, too. I know this is not a popular thing to say, but I also know that those who most adamantly oppose change are the ones least likely to read this book! It's up to those of us who truly care about the future of our deer to demand change, changes that will benefit the long-term health and well-being of our deer. For this ever to take place, a lot of thinking will have to be adjusted.

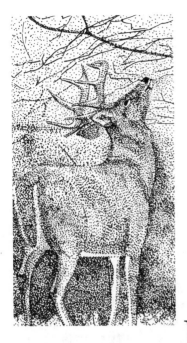

10

Poaching:
Deer at Any Cost

Nobody seems to agree on exactly what poaching is or just how severe a problem it is. And nobody seems to agree what penalties poachers should suffer. *The American Heritage Dictionary* defines poaching: "(1) to trespass on another's property in order to take fish or game; (2) to take fish or game in a forbidden area." The same dictionary defines a poacher as "a person who hunts or fishes illegally on the property of another." *The Encyclopedia Britannica* defines poaching: "in law, the shooting, trapping, or taking of game or fish from private property or from a place where such practices are specially reserved or forbidden."

There is a problem with these definitions, stemming from their old English origins. In England the landowners own the animals on their land. They do not belong to the state, as they do in America. There, poaching was a crime against the landowner, so the landowner himself could not be a poacher.

Michigan's DNR has a profile of poachers. Based on actual violators arrested, the poacher is most likely to be a white male in his early twenties, with little or no advanced education, who works at a menial, perhaps part-time, job or who may well be an unemployed transient. The advantage of a profile is that it may help law enforcement personnel key in on an individual who merits scrutiny. The disadvantage is that a profile may serve as a blinder, which limits the perception of the obvious. A well-known, well-respected older person who may be acting just as suspiciously may be overlooked because he doesn't fit the profile.

My three-year study has opened my eyes in many ways; the area of poaching is a particularly clear example. I am now convinced that, next to the destruction and degradation of habitat, poaching is the biggest single threat to our wildlife populations. I do not believe the DNR is even remotely cognizant of just how huge a problem poaching represents. Over the last twelve years, the DNR has repeatedly demonstrated its lack of effort, concern, or even interest in addressing poaching. Furthermore, if the area of my study is representative, the DNR's profile of a poacher is way off base. This assertion is based not on idle speculation, but on my own firsthand observation.

How many readers are aware that poaching has no legal meaning in the state of Michigan? Poaching is not defined by statute, common law, or executive order in Michigan, so no one is ever convicted of poaching by a Michigan court. For clarity, in the remainder of this book I'll consider poaching to be: (1) the killing of deer outside the limits of the legally set deer seasons; (2) killing more than the legally prescribed bag limits; and (3) killing or attempting to kill deer during nighttime hours.

Before my study I never would have believed what I now know to be true: in the area I observed, there are more deer poached than there are taken legally! Throughout 1991, I saw or became aware of twenty-six deer that had died in one way or another. In four of these cases I could not determine the cause of death. Nine deer had been hit by vehicles, thirteen had been shot. Of the thirteen shot, ten were bucks, two were does, and one could not be sexed because all I found was a gut pile, partially eaten by a fox. Using my definition of poaching, of the thirteen animals shot, I believe only six were legally taken and seven were poached. The seven poached were all bucks.

What's amazing is just how brazen poachers can be. In late February 1991, I went to a local bank and ran into one of the most blatant poachers I know. We talked briefly about the past deer season, and then he got a wry smile on his face and said, "I ain't done yet—too damned many deer around here; I better take one, maybe two, before they starve to death. You know, just to help thin the herd a little!" I left without saying much, but I decided to keep an eye on his property for the next few days.

On February 26, I was heading in that direction when I jumped thirteen deer off a neighbor's property. They ran onto the poacher's property, with me trailing slowly behind. About five minutes later, I heard two shots fired directly in front of the poacher's house. I waited a couple hours before going onto his property to look around (I had previously gotten permission to go on his property). I found nothing that day or the next, but on February 28, I found a button buck that had been shot and quartered—rear quarters only—less than two hundred yards from the man's house.

In 1992, I knew of thirty-three deer that had died. In three cases I could not determine the cause, nine had been hit by vehicles, and twenty-one had been shot. Of the twenty-one shot, seventeen were bucks, three were does, and one I couldn't sex. Using my definition, I believe that no fewer than fifteen—all bucks—had been poached. Why?

Obviously I do not hear of every single deer that is taken, poached, killed accidentally, or lost by natural causes. But I live in a small rural community where people talk about what goes on and everyone knows about everyone else. Hunters who take deer legally usually tell others, and deer/car accidents are a frequent topic of conversation. And in addition to scouring every inch of my study area on foot, I have had help from a couple of low-key, well-liked, non-threatening informants who are very much in touch with the local scene. If anything, the true number of poached deer is higher than the ones I know about, not lower!

In 1993, I knew of nineteen deer that had died: seven were hit by vehicles, nine were shot, and in three cases I couldn't determine the cause of death. Using my definition, I believe that five of the nine shot were poached (four bucks and one doe). The poachers of the doe were caught, and, ironically, in this case they fit the DNR's profile of a poacher strikingly.

Psychologists tell us that all human beings go through stages of growth and development, with different areas or facets of our lives developing at different rates. Development is full of pitfalls, which may cause some areas to slow down or stop developing altogether. Psychologists refer to such deviant development as "arrests" in development, "retardation," or "regression."

Regardless of the label used, these developmental glitches affect us all; no one develops fully mature responses in every aspect of his or her life. Examples are all around us. The strong, healthy, self-sufficient adult who, when physically ill with the flu, suddenly reverts to the whining, complaining, helpless six-year-old child. The responsible, cool-headed business executive who, upon leaving the office and getting behind the wheel of a car, suddenly reverts to the impulsive adolescent he was twenty years before.

The same kind of thing occurs among hunters. A normal, level-headed, law-abiding hunter sees a big, beautiful ten-point buck three days before season, and he can't resist temptation. Suddenly, we've got a poacher. Psychologists say hunters go through a stage where numbers—or size—of animals is all that counts. I believe that is the stage where a hunter's normal development may cease, and he becomes a poacher.

While I would never assert that all hunters are poachers, it is a sad fact that every poacher I've known was also a hunter. During my three years of field study, I've had a chance to identify the poachers in my neighborhood, and a majority of them are nowhere near the Michigan DNR's profile of a poacher. Here's what I've found:

1. Poaching runs in families. It's a generational thing: Dad did it (or does it), so I'll do it, too
2. Chronological age is not a determining factor. I know poachers as young as fourteen, and I know one in his seventies

3. Apparently, gender is important. Every poacher I've known is male

4. A poacher is unlikely to stop—even if caught and arrested several times! One of my neighbors has been caught three times and is still poaching. It seems to become a game of one-upmanship (I killed more—or bigger—than you!) where winning is more important than following the rules

5. Over time, a poacher's activity seems to increase in frequency; I've never seen it decrease

6. Poachers commonly express outrage at other poachers without (apparently) being aware of the parallel with their own behavior

7. Poachers often try to justify their actions. Two of the most blatant poachers I know of are quite wealthy and own large expanses of land. Typically, they rationalize, "If it weren't for me feeding them, the deer wouldn't even be here!" Or, "There's too damn many deer anyway. I'm gonna do everyone a favor and take one or two." Of course, during hunting season, they sing a different tune: "Damn DNR gives out too many doe permits—ain't no damn deer left!"

8. The most serious violators poach early in the fall. They want to be sure they kill that buck (or those bucks) before legitimate, law-abiding hunters ever get a chance at them

9. Most of the poachers I've known were out-and-out braggarts. They made no bones about the number and size of the animals taken—though they vehemently deny they got them by poaching

10. Whether seasoned veterans or young ones who've learned from their elders, the poachers I know work pretty much alone and shoot only bucks. They'd never shoot a doe, and most are incensed to think that anyone else would, either

11. Poachers seem to have an inordinate fascination with deer. They spend a lot of time watching and talking about them, but their knowledge is very limited, and often their interest lies in only one thing—killing them!

12. At least in rural communities like mine, poachers are seldom fooling anyone. Many of my neighbors talk openly about who the poachers are. One neighbor even has a video he took of a deer being poached. A teller at my bank said to me one day, "I hear your neighbors are up to their old tricks again." Everyone knows who is poaching, but no one is willing to come forward about it. One of my neighbors, though not a poacher himself, is rabid in his dislike of poachers— except for one poacher: his best friend!

I sometimes chuckle about how incensed big-time poachers can get over trespassers on their land. It's not that I condone trespassing—because I certainly don't—but the poachers' behavior is far worse than the behavior they're complaining about!

Poachers steal from all of us just as assuredly as do bank robbers. There's no reasonable excuse to justify such behaviors, and there's no justification for hunters to turn their backs on the problem. You are either going to be part of the problem or part of the solution, there is no in between.

I believe poaching is most likely to be a problem in communities that are undergoing rapid, significant change (this includes most communities, of course). My study area and the areas immediately surrounding are in the midst of tremendous growth. The human population has nearly tripled in the past twenty-five years, and it's still growing. The type of resident has changed, too. There are fewer farmers and more people who moved from the city. And there's rapid mobility, i.e., people moving frequently from one place to another. The percentage of long-term residents is much lower than in the past.

I believe all these factors create a psychological isolation from the land and its animals, both for the long-term residents still there and for the newcomers, who couldn't yet have developed an affinity for the local environment. The increase in poaching is, I believe, just one of the repercussions of the marked social change.

I'm aware of the danger of overgeneralizing, but I'm struck by the adolescent character of the behavior I see in the poachers I know: preoccupation with motor vehicles (they like to work on their own vehicles even though they could pay to have it done), reckless driving at excessive speeds, physical altercations (fights in bars, fights over girlfriends, brawls at beach parties), and bragging. These aren't kids. They're thirty-, forty-, fifty-year-old men!

As if the poaching situation were not bad enough, what's even more discouraging is what happens when you try to do something about it. During the past ten years or so, I have on at least six occasions called (or tried to call) the DNR to report shots being fired after dark near my home. The shortest response time? Forty-five minutes! Trying to get a quicker response, I've called my local police, the county sheriff, or the state police several times. Although I live within a leisurely ten- or twelve-minute drive from these police stations, the shortest time it has taken them to respond is an hour. On numerous occasions, to the best of my knowledge, they never responded at all! Sometimes, I learned, they just relayed the information to the DNR, who, in turn, did nothing.

In disgust over my failure to get anyone to make even an honest attempt at catching poachers—or even to strike some fear into them—for several years I gave up. Then, near the end of the 1993 gun season, I was talking to a friend who is a district biologist with the DNR about some poaching I had observed and my frustration over trying to get official response. He gave me the name and phone number of the head of a major division of the law enforcement section of the DNR, who turned out to be very articulate and seemed genuinely interested. We talked for nearly an hour, and he promised me he'd take charge of the case personally. That was eighteen months ago, and I haven't heard from him since.

I fully believe that hunters are a product of our culture and times and that our behaviors reflect those of our society as a whole. I live on a side road that runs off a major highway. If you drive the speed limit on that highway, you'll be run over by almost every other vehicle on the road. Nobody, it seems, drives within the constraints of the law.

I live in a county that has a Sunday hunting closure law (you may hunt only your own or state land on Sunday)—yet beyond any doubt there is more hunting near my home by nonlandowners on Sunday than on any other day of the week. Two days before the 1993 gun season, I found a neighbor building a tree stand along the edge of one of his cornfields. Since you may not hunt from an elevated stand during Michigan's gun season—and knowing this neighbor wasn't building the stand for an archery hunt—I confronted him about it. He looked at me in a highly indignant manner and said, "I always hunt from a tree stand!"

Since there are so many scoff-laws in our society as a whole, I suppose it should come as no surprise that hunting has its share. But there is a bitter reality that hunters better wake up to. Driving in this country is not likely to be outlawed in our lifetimes, and shopping (hence shoplifting) will never cease, but if hunting is someday outlawed altogether, we'll have no one but ourselves to blame. If we want hunting to continue, it's our duty not only to obey the law ourselves but to see to it that our peers do.

11

Why Hunting Is Important

In the next couple of chapters, despite the fact that this is not a hunting book, I will try to clarify the relationships between wildlife management and hunting and poaching, as well as to answer some important but little understood realities about hunting and wildlife. I'll also address what is perhaps the most important question of all facing wildlife and wildlife-related groups today: Is hunting necessary in today's society, do we need to hunt? While this may seem to digress from the focus of a book detailing the life and behaviors of the white-tailed deer, believe me it does not. The reality is that without management, and a surefire method to finance it, there would be no white-tailed deer to manage, at least as far as we recognize them today. Management issues then are not tangential but rather central, and paramount to the whole question of whether or not we're to have healthy wildlife populations. It's therefore absolutely vital that anyone with an interest in wildlife understand all the nuances that this entails.

Not many people understand the profound differences between legitimate hunting and poaching. I believe they need to be spelled out. Hunting is an emotional issue. The purposeful, intentional taking of life demands nothing less.

But hunting in this country is a legitimate, legally sanctioned activity. If you don't agree with that there are legal avenues for you to pursue in an attempt to try and change it, and that's fine, that is your right. In the meantime, at least let's try to understand the profound differences between hunting and the parasitic, destructive activity of poaching. Make no mistake about it, poaching, in any of its various forms, is an illegal, unlawful activity.

Game management departments have very few "tools" of management at their disposal. Two of their most powerful are habitat manipulation and the setting of hunting guidelines. Timbering leases, on state-owned lands, are tendered with stipulations about the total footage of lumber to be taken; the manner in which the timber is taken; the time frame in which it's taken; and the restoration of the land after it's taken. Additionally, sometimes other types of habitat manipulations are made other than timbering. There's the creation of food plots in some cases, and there's flooding of certain lands, at designated times (done mostly for waterfowl), for example. It should be apparent that state lands, and/or federal lands, in most states form but a very small percentage of the total land mass; therefore, the various states have really very little control of overall land management. Most state management departments will, if asked by the landowner, offer suggestions, ideas, and make recommendations regarding management practices, but they cannot (unless the activities involved violate wetlands or pollution statutes) insist it be done that way, and most landowners never ask. The bottom line is that game departments have relatively little impact on habitat manipulation on a statewide basis.

By doing all manner of economically feasible studies, game departments come up with population figures of various game animals that they desire to carry from one year to the next. These figures are designed, ideally to: (1) insure that the so-called breeding stock necessary to continue the healthy and viable perpetuation of the population is protected; (2) allow the habitat, without damage, to carry that proposed population; and (3) to do so without the starvation or deprivation of the population in question. The game department then attempts to reach the proposed population levels by the setting and manipulation of various hunting rules and regulations under its control. These include chiefly: season duration, daily bag limits, season limits, and sex of the animals taken (when/where appropriate). Most other hunting rules and regulations concern safety-related issues.

People have such irrational notions of what game management is that, if it weren't so tragic, it would almost be funny. At the end of each day, or at the beginning of each difficult time period for the animals, the DNR simply moves in, packs them up, and waits for more benign conditions to reign before releasing them again, right? The reality is that essentially the only actual management that DNR biologists can accomplish is that done through hunting.

As you can easily see, since habitat manipulation is so severely restricted, the most important management tool game departments have at their disposal is that of hunting. Besides being the "fuel" behind attaining management goals, hunting is the "economic fuel," too. Game department budgets do not come out of the states' general revenue funds, but rather directly from license sales—hunting, fishing, and trapping—and from the federal government in the form of Pittman-Robertson funds. This 1938 act, properly titled the Federal Aid in Wildlife Restoration Act (Pittman-Robertson Act, for the two men who sponsored it), has generated more than two billion dollars for wildlife management programs since its inception. States get three dollars for each dollar they put into the program. The program demands that all sporting license fees generated by the state must go directly into the administration of the state fish and game department(s). The federal revenues are generated from a 13 percent excise tax on outdoor-related equipment sales—chiefly hunting (guns and ammunition) and fishing equipment. These federally raised funds are for the express purpose of game management.

Therefore, law-abiding hunters are the various state game departments' biggest allies. It's through hunters, and their willing adherence to the law, that game departments can meaningfully manage their wildlife. Hunters, by way of check stations, questionnaires and surveys, render vital statistics to game departments regarding numbers of animals taken, the condition of those animals, and the overall health, age, sex, and well-being of those populations. Without hunters, as game department financing and operations are now set up, there would be no meaningful game management in this country.

What do poachers offer game management? Nothing but headaches! They make the accurate, meaningful tallying of kill figures nearly impossible to compute (they don't register their illicit activities). They not only don't contribute financially (poachers don't buy licenses as legitimate hunters do) to game management, they steal from it, since their activities demand that a larger segment of game department budgets be spent on law enforcement rather than on management. They also steal directly from all of us. Poachers, like any other criminal element, cost us all, while contributing nothing.

For those who believe hunting should be outlawed, and that the killing of animals is wrong, I'd like for them to answer, or at least think about, the following questions. If game department budgets come from hunter-raised revenues, and never come out of the states' general revenue

Just as today's hunters must face up to their less-than-honorable behaviors, so too must the antihunters. The claims and the assertions of antihunters are absolutely outrageous! They'd like everyone to buy into their zany notions that the world is an idyllic place for wildlife. It is not! Today's populations must be controlled—that, whether they choose to deal with it or not, is a given. The real issue is whether we do it wisely in the future, with the very best interests of the animals in mind, or whether we continue down the same dangerous pathway we have been on until now.

coffers, how would you propose that wildlife management be financed should hunting be eliminated? In these days of multimillion dollar government deficits, no one can possibly believe that the various state governments would fund programs for management if hunting dollars were eliminated. And, let us not forget that the federal Pittman-Robertson funds (representing a huge percentage of all state game departments' funding) are tied directly to state-raised funds; if state-raised funds, earmarked specifically for wildlife management, dry up or dwindle, so do federal funds. Why, you might ask, does wildlife need to be managed? Didn't they do just fine, for eons, before man took it upon himself to "manage" them? To answer these questions requires a brief history lesson.

Primitive man, so far as we can tell, has always hunted, and there's every reason to believe that he almost always did so with an eye to conserving the breeding stocks of the animals that he depended upon. It was essentially only after other peoples moved into foreign areas (really the eighteenth and nineteenth centuries), that animal populations were subjected to pressures they could not sustain. With some notable exceptions in Africa and parts of Asia (always born out of government lethargy and/or greed), it was never "sport" hunting that caused animal population declines. Most definitely, this was the case throughout all of North America. There has never been a North American animal population put into jeopardy because of recreational hunting. In fact, if it weren't for the concerned actions and demands of North American sportsmen, God only knows what would have happened to North America's wildlife. All one needs to understand the truth of that is to know a little about the history of development on this continent.

No one came to this country, until at least the late 1800s, to hunt for recreation. Subsistence hunting and market hunting were what everyone practiced, from the time of the pilgrims to the end of pioneering days. For these people trying to eke a living out of the wilderness, there were no rules, no laws, no seasons, no limits. They took what they wanted or needed, when they wanted or needed it. Finally, by the mid-1800s there were a few wealthy individuals, from southern plantation owners to wealthy northern land barons and industrialists, who began to hunt for sport.

What these men (and a few women) discovered shocked them. The woods, fields, lakes, and rivers of their youth that had abounded with game suddenly had none. Market hunting—an activity where hunters killed as much game as they possibly could, with no laws regulating numbers, seasons, sex, or anything else, and sold what they killed to the market place—supplied the needs of the developing young nation. The demands of New York City, Philadelphia, Pittsburgh, Richmond, Cleveland, Detroit, Chicago, the list goes on and on, were seemingly insatiable, but animal numbers were not. It's hard for us today to envision bison and elk as far east as Pennsylvania; or grizzly bear as far east as the Mississippi; or wolves all along the eastern seaboard; or trout in the rivers around New York City, but that's the way it had been. What market hunting didn't exterminate, pollution and habitat destruction did. People were so busy carving a living from this new land, and "conquering" the wilderness, that no one gave any thought to the destruction it was causing. No one, that is, until the advent, in the mid to late eighteenth century, of "sportsmen."

These sportsmen were wealthy, powerful and well positioned. They began to fight to bring an end to market hunting and for restrictions upon their own hunting and fishing. They began to push for laws regulating when, how, and how many animals could be taken. They also fought for laws that would raise revenues by taxing themselves as sportsmen, so monies for enforcement of game law violations would be available. It was an uphill battle. For thirty, forty, even fifty years the progress was extremely slow, as our animal populations continued to plummet.

The darkest days were those of the very late 1800s and the early 1900s. The white-tailed deer, mule deer, pronghorn antelope, elk, bison, moose, woodland caribou, grizzly, black bear, beaver, otter, most waterfowl, the passenger pigeon, cranes and egrets, and many more animals were either gone or in extreme jeopardy. It is a grave oversight to believe that anyone, other than hunters and fishermen, cared. The real turning point came when Theodore

Roosevelt was elected president in 1900. President Roosevelt was one of those early pioneers of the sportsmen's movement in this country. Finally, from his pulpit as president, he could see to it that many of the changes for which he'd fought so long became reality. The Lacey Act of 1900 finally eliminated market hunting in the United States. In 1918, the Migratory Bird Treaty Act between the United States and Canada (joined by Mexico in 1937) enabled waterfowl management to have real meaning. In 1934, the Migratory Bird Hunting Stamp Act began raising revenues—by taxing hunters—for the express purpose of waterfowl habitat improvement and protection. In 1937, the Pittman-Robertson Federal Aid in Wildlife Restoration Act began raising revenues through the excise tax on sportsmen mentioned earlier.

It must also be pointed out that there was no such thing as "wildlife management" until Aldo Leopold, the "father" of wildlife management, published his text *Game Management* in 1933. Even then, the "science" of management was nothing more than an insightful set of beliefs about what could be done; there was no meaningful data to back it up. Leopold, and those who have followed him, then set about refining the notions of management, and collecting data. The results have been dramatic; management is a reality today. We now have the expertise to manage many of the wildlife problems we're faced with, but they take money; as I've pointed out, without hunting that money wouldn't exist.

There are many in the antihunting movement who would have you believe that wildlife management, as it's practiced today, is nothing more than "game management." Their contention is that somehow habitats are manipulated to create more animals so that hunters then will have plenty of targets to shoot at. I'll address that argument by saying that in those few cases where that does occur it is ethically wrong and must cease. Wildlife agencies should not be allowed to perpetuate animals simply for hunters to shoot; if it's done, where it's done, it's wrong. The reality the antihunters don't want you to know, however, is that is seldom done. They have this unrealistic notion that it's somehow possible to create habitat, stock it with X number of animals, and those animals will then live in harmony forever with their habitat. That's absolutely absurd! Animals, like people, have this nasty little habit of breeding and producing offspring.

Like it or not, mankind has profoundly altered habitats and ecosystems to the point that we now must manage the populations that are in them. The only alternative is to let the animals die of every other cause imaginable, for it's a fact that every animal born must die. If we were to manage in that manner the animals would first destroy their habitat before they'd then succumb to disease and starvation. The notion that many in the antihunting community have that it is somehow more "noble" or "natural" for a wild animal to die of disease or starvation than to die at the hands of a hunter is absolutely absurd. Mankind has always hunted; we evolved as a predatory species. What on earth is suddenly "unnatural" about us killing? They often use the trite argument that mankind has evolved beyond that point, but that's equally absurd. Mankind has evolved as a predator for two to three million years; just because for the past few hundred we haven't had to hunt to survive they'd like us to believe that hunting is no longer ingrained in us? That's ridiculous. I go back to the original question about where revenues for management would come from—should hunting be eliminated? I've never heard any realistic answer to that.

There is another issue I'd like to address and that's the term most generally applied to hunting today—"sport" hunting. I suggest we abandon the use of that term once and for all. There is absolutely nothing about hunting that makes it a sport. The intentional, willful killing of an animal should never be done with the sense of sport in mind. Sport is an activity in which both, or all, participants have, or should have, an equal chance of victory. What chance do the animals we hunt have of winning? If they survive our onslaught today, will they tomorrow? Escape cannot be equated with victory! I'm a hunter, have been all my life, and I've every intention of continuing for as long as I can. But hunting for me is an activity, a recreation. It is something I practice, it is something I strive to do efficiently and with the most knowledge and skill I can bring to bare. I kill.

I have no reason, since I do so legally and with the upmost respect for the animals I hunt, to apologize for that. But I do not do so in the name of sport. You'd better believe that if I for one moment believed that the animals I hunt had the same chance of winning as I do, and that their winning meant my death, I'd never hunt again. Yet, ironically, the animals do win because I hunt. I'm one of those who helps finance their habitat needs, and helps control their population so the threats of disease, reduced fertility, and starvation are lessened for them.

12

Hunting and Ethics

In the winter of 1995 the Michigan Department of Natural Resources (DNR) held public hearings on the issue of "baiting" while deer hunting. For those not familiar with the practice of baiting I'll explain it. Baiting is the act of a "hunter" taking any of several deer "foods" to a site in the woods or fields where he (she) intends to "hunt," and placing it there with the hope of attracting the deer. (Baiting is legal in some states, illegal in many, legal for some types of hunting, illegal for many more and, by federal statute, always illegal, anywhere, for hunting waterfowl.) The "hunter" will most often do this at least several days prior to actually sitting over the bait, with the hope that the deer will discover the bait and begin using it regularly. In Michigan, until the late 1960s, while being legal, baiting was almost never practiced. But because of new technologies in archery hunting equipment, and hence widespread increases in the numbers of archers, baiting became widespread. Soon those that baited while archery "hunting" began using the practice while rifle "hunting" as well. In the late 1960s, it's estimated that fewer than 5 percent of

Michigan hunters practiced baiting. The latest figures are absolutely shocking to me; the DNR estimates that during the 1994 deer seasons some 75 percent of archers and 56 percent of gun hunters practiced baiting. The entire issue is very volatile. Those who bait see nothing wrong with the practice; those who don't are incensed by it. There's rarely any middle ground.

I attended a couple of the public hearings. In one of them I almost immediately recognized an old friend, and went to sit with him. This gentleman was, I guess, an interested bystander, much as I was. But considering his background, his presence was more than just that of an average citizen. This man is a former state senator, and a former member of the Natural Resources Commission in Michigan. (The Michigan governor has the authority during his tenure to appoint members to this commission, which has seven members appointed for four-year terms. The NRC is the public policy making vehicle that oversees the DNR—it dictates DNR goals and policy.) Most of those who spoke at the hearing were either for or against the practice of baiting, and they put forth the same old tired arguments that are always aired about the matter.

But, as I sat with this former (and would be again!) politician, one gentleman stood forward and hit the nail on the head: "Baiting is ethically wrong, and I believe that everyone in this room knows exactly what would happen to baiting if the issue was put forth to the electorate of this state." Well, my old friend went nuts: "See, this is what this is going to turn into. I don't want this to become an ethical issue!" Well, my friend, it is an ethical issue, pure and simple. Despite all the absurd arguments, both for and against baiting, it is indeed an ethical issue. The spokesman who said he knew, we all knew, the outcome if baiting were "put forth to the electorate" was absolutely correct. The fact that the politician didn't have the guts to take a stand explains why politicians are held in such contempt today. The general populace knows, even if the majority of hunters do not, that shooting deer over a bait pile is not hunting!

We live in a strange world, a world that lacks respect, a world that lacks morals, a world of instant, self-centered gratification, a world of rudeness, a world that lacks ethics, a world of insensitivity, a world of total disregard for other's feelings. I attended a meeting with one of my sons recently, at a school that he'll attend in the future. As I sat in the audience trying to hear the speaker, three teen-age girls sat in the row in front of us; they were so loud and obnoxious that I could not hear what was being said. Their parents were sitting there with them and never once attempted to quiet them down. Such is commonplace in our society today; should we expect that hunters would behave any different-ly? To my friend the politician, and to all others as well, I'll say we'd better.

Hunting in this country is a privilege, and it seems very evident to me that it's a privilege in dire jeopardy. With each year that passes we see more and more areas closed to hunting, more and more legal battles contested, and more and more losses. Even when hunters "win" these battles, they do so with slimmer and slimmer margins of victory, always building animosities along the way. Dealing with people as I do, almost daily on hunting-related issues and topics, I'm appalled at the stories I hear, and the attitudes so many have.

I appeared recently as a guest speaker at a sportsmen's club in Canada, and during the course of the evening was approached by a gentleman who said he was familiar with the area where I live, since he had some friends who lived near there. He then went on to say that these friends of his were rather poverty stricken, and that he knew we must have a good deer population, because they certainly didn't have any trouble getting one whenever they needed it! I had purposely been selected by the superintendent of a park in that area of Canada as the guest speaker because of my photographic work, and because of my strong stand against hunting violators. I was dumfounded, I didn't even know what to say to this man.

Just this past weekend my family and I went to north-ern Michigan, to the area where our elk herd is concentrat-ed. There's a resort in the area that provides sleigh rides into the elk country itself, and we took it. It was wonderful, and one of the things that made it particularly enjoyable to me was the young lady who acted as our guide. She was very well-spoken, very knowledgeable, and seemed to have great respect for the wildlife. Near the end of the ride, however, as she and I talked, she completely blew it. She preceded to tell me that while poaching of elk is uncommon (since the fines are so high), poaching of deer and especially of turkeys is common, due to the ease with which they can be poached. She laughed and said, "With turkeys, you know, you kill 'em and eat 'em the same night!" I can't be sure, but the way she said it made me believe that if she didn't do this herself, at the very least she saw nothing wrong with it. For the life of me, I cannot understand such an attitude in anyone. The rationalization so often heard, "So long as they use the meat, I don't see anything wrong with it," is garbage. Would these same people condone the stealing of meat from a grocery, just because it wasn't wasted? It's absurd; poaching is thievery, pure and simple, and cannot be condoned under any circumstances.

On that same little trip, I took my family to show them a waterfall in the area. As we neared the area of the falls we drove past a rural farm house; hanging from a tree in the front yard of the house were four coyotes. Now there's nothing wrong with trappers or hunters legally taking coyote, but why on earth, when they know how sensitive a lot of people are regarding the killing of any animal, do they feel the need to hang the carcasses in full view of a busy roadway? That's the very kind of insensitivity that jeopardizes all hunting.

Whether hunters like it or not, hunting is a very highly scrutinized activity in our society. Personally, I believe this is right; the taking of a life, any life, should be deeply questioned, and closely monitored. And, from all my experiences dealing with people, most of them are willing to concede that there's a place for hunting, so long as it's done ethically. To most people I believe this means several things: hunting only when the population in question can sustain the loss; hunting in a manner that is the least disruptive to the population; hunting in an unobtrusive manner (those who don't hunt don't want to see the dead animals); and hunting only under legally set guidelines, that take into account all of the the biological needs of the animal.

This philosophy puts added responsibility on game departments, too, that many clearly have been unwilling to acknowledge and accept. Game departments can be, and sometimes have been, as unethical as the hunters that they've tried to satisfy. Game populations should never, under any circumstances, be manipulated to produce excess numbers just so hunters can have additional targets. One specific example that comes to mind is a now defunct program that the Michigan DNR had for several years. It was called "put and take." It was a pheasant-rearing program, run by the state, wherein pen-raised pheasant, which the state knew were incapable of surviving in the wild, were released into well-marked areas on state land. Hunters then were free to come in, within a couple of hours of the time of release, and hunt these birds. That is wholly unethical and I can't believe the state ever got into such a fiasco, but it did.

I firmly believe it is far easier to contest the common arguments against hunting than it is those against hunters. Until I hear sound, rational alternatives (and I don't believe there are any) to the issues raised in Chapter 11, I firmly believe hunting does indeed have a place: it has a rich heritage; it is an essential "tool" in population control; it is, or darned well better be, biologically justifiable, whenever/wherever allowed; it is just as important for many people today as it has ever been, despite the fact that perhaps today we don't have to hunt, from a survivalist perspective. I also believe that when hunters are accused of poor, unethical, ignorant, insensitive behaviors, the accusers are usually correct.

Beyond any doubt, hunters are under the gun. If hunting is to survive, they'd darned well better clean up their act. They must become more responsible; they need to become a lot more knowledgeable; and they need to become much more responsive in dealing with the issues that confront hunting. The real tragedy we're going to have to deal with as a nation if hunting is ever banned is not the lost opportunity for hunters; rather it's the loss of wildlife. For as irrational as it may sound superficially, I honestly don't believe we can have healthy wildlife populations without hunting. It's something we all need to think about.

Our deer—and all our animal populations—deserve nothing less than the best we can do for them. Like it or not, there are no viable, economic alternatives to what hunting can accomplish, and already has accomplished. Through hunter-generated revenues we've brought back the wood duck, the egrets, the bison, the pronghorn, the whitetail and many more from the very brink of oblivion. But we must continue to look for answers, and we must do even better in the future. Hunters, those who truly care about the future of wildlife, must begin to face the issues that threaten their activity *now*—tomorrow may well be too late.

Section III

13

Distribution and Activity Levels Throughout the Year

When I began this project, one of my primary objectives was to determine as precisely as I could the ways in which deer relate to their habitat throughout the year. Anyone who spends time watching deer soon realizes that you don't see deer in June, for example, in the same areas or at the same times of day that you see them in February. I wanted to understand why.

Is it because the deer actually use different areas at these times or is it simply easier to see them at certain times of the year—when there's snow pack or when the foliage is down, for example? Or do they use the same areas but at different times of day that change with the seasons? Do shifts in the deer's habits correspond to the seasons, as we think of seasons, or are they determined by other factors?

To answer these questions I knew that I'd need to devote an immense amount of time to field study—in the swamps, in the woods, in the crop fields—and that I'd need detailed recordings of my observations on a daily basis year-round in order to bolster an imperfect memory and detect shifts in the deer behaviors over time.

I began by making detailed maps of my study area that showed all plots of land and the type of cover on each. Every day I recorded and dated all sign observed. I had thought I'd make a new map for each season, but I realized that biased the data in favor of seasons as man defines them, not deer, so I decided instead to make a new map whenever I noticed a major, consistent change in the deer's behavior.

Next, I made detailed daily notes of all the activity I observed. I hereby publicly apologize to my wife and kids for ignoring them for long periods at the end of each day as I frantically recorded each detail before it was forgotten! My observations included much more than just a cursory examination of sign—I included pellet counts (when appropriate, as I'll explain later), runway examinations and counts, assessment of crop damage, bedding site counts, browsing activity, and literally anything and everything else that came to my attention.

Finally, I recorded where I saw the deer, the date and time, and detailed weather information. It turned out that it is meaningful to divide deer behavior roughly into the same four seasons experienced by man, with the possible exception of spring. The changes deer normally undergo in spring are dependent upon weather changes and, of course, these may not coincide precisely with our calendar.

WINTER

As I explained at the beginning of this book, one of my motivations for study was that I often see deer behaviors that don't agree with descriptions given by other deer researchers around the country. In describing the deer's use of the land in winter, I have to confront such a discrepancy right off the bat.

It's long been accepted that once cold weather sets in, the deer's daily movements, general travel patterns, and level of feeding activity all decrease dramatically. "Up to 40 percent" is the figure often given. My observations show that this is a misleading oversimplification. Actually, several factors determine whether a decrease occurs: (1) sufficient previous cold weather for the deer to have become acclimated to cold (most often in southern Michigan this is not the case); (2) how deep the snow pack, if any; and (3) the amount of food available to the deer.

What I observed all three years of my study was a tremendous *flurry* of activity whenever temperatures plummeted around the end of the year. This increased activity occurred as early as December 15 (1990) and as late as December 25 (1993), and it always corresponded to a sudden, dramatic drop in temperature.

Furthermore, this heightened activity was observable across the board. Increased feeding was witnessed in the deer's usage of crop fields and stands of oaks (when—and only when—mast was present). Long-distance movements were witnessed in their road-crossing frequency and use of pasture land. Increased usage of all types of cover and habitat was noted, although if it was cold enough for the swamplands to freeze (which it was all three years), the deer were beginning to withdraw from the swamps. During this increased activity, more deer were seen.

What I believe this demonstrates, more than anything else, is that when winter comes on rapidly, the deer's

Winter, especially in the North, is very hard on our deer. I photographed this doe as she was eating shards of bark from this cherry tree. Despite her good appearance, that's starvation food!

metabolism (and psyche, as well?) is simply not ready for it yet, and they get cold and increase their activity to generate warmth. But whether this hypothesis is right or wrong, my observations are indisputable: under the conditions described, early winter brings an increase in activity, not a decrease. I'm willing to agree that if winter were to come on very gradually—which it almost never does in southern Michigan—perhaps we would see the dramatic decrease in deer activity widely described by others.

My hypothesis about cold stimulating activity seems to be born out by a comparison between rutting activity levels in southern Michigan and the U.P. I've always felt that rutting activity in southern Michigan is just not as exaggerated and extreme or intense as it is in the Upper Peninsula. Could it be that the greater rutting activity we see in the Upper Peninsula and other cold environs is a result of lack of acclimation to newly arrived cold, in combination with effects of the rut? I think it's very likely.

The heightened activity levels I've witnessed around the end of the year last for about two or three weeks, after which there *is* a rapid decrease in activity level. All three years of my study showed this decrease beginning around the middle of January; however, the decrease depended very much on the depth of snow pack present and the weather. In 1991, we had roughly ten inches of snow by mid-January, and deer movement and activity really plummeted. In 1992, we had very little snow pack and lots of snow-free areas, and the deer activity levels, while decreasing from those exhibited earlier, were much higher than in 1991. I believe that snow depth influences activity level more than any other factor during early winter in southern Michigan. Wind velocity and temperature come next.

What happens when snow pack is present after the deer have become acclimated to winter conditions—after, say, mid-January? Once again my findings differ, at least to a degree, from what we read. If it's cold (nighttime lows below the twenties, with daytime highs in the twenties or low thirties) and there's at least three inches of snow, what I saw was a gradual decrease in all forms of movement. Long-range movement decreases rapidly and dramatically, the amount and variety of habitat utilized decreases, and feeding decreases.

Once acclimation has occurred, the rapidity of these changes depends on the severity of the weather. If conditions are severe, the changes may occur within a week. If the weather worsens gradually (unusual), the changes may take two or three weeks.

What precisely are these changes? I usually covered about one-half square mile of my study area each day. I found the swamps and areas with shallow standing water (flood plain or flooded fields) were vacated first. If there was no mast present, the open oaks were the next to lose the deer. As late January moves into February, activity declines gradually but steadily in all crop fields. Feeding in general declines quite dramatically. This is the time when the 40 percent figure often cited appears to be accurate for southern Michigan.

Throughout the time these changes are occurring, usage of shielded and protected areas increases, and movements outside these areas—thick, brushy areas, areas with scattered but numerous pines, hilly areas with thick cover—decreases steadily. By late January, if there's snow cover of five inches or more and temperatures are mostly below freezing, the deer will be fairly isolated within these pockets. For the three consecutive winters it turned out that within my study area of about five square miles, there were seven such areas and over 90 percent of the deer were in those seven areas at any given time. The more winter drags on and the more severe the weather, the smaller these areas become; eventually, the use of the fringe and the short excursions made by the deer earlier stop altogether.

The DNR's observation that deer in southern Michigan do not "yard up" as they do farther north does not square with my findings, which clearly show that they do if the weather is severe enough (all three years of my study). If the weather breaks—and this is important—if snow depth decreases or melts entirely, the deer immediately break out of these areas and occupy a much larger fraction of their available range. The deer's reaction to snow and cold in late winter is strikingly different from that of early winter. In late winter, they waste no time in getting back into the smaller, well-protected areas—they are there within hours!

Back in the 1940s Michigan biologist Ilo "Bart" Bartlett called deer yards "ghettos." I see no difference in the deer's desire to break out of them, whether in northern Iron County or southern Lapeer County. The obvious difference is that in the south deer never starve in their yards. Also, they're not confined to them for nearly as long as the northern deer. But it's obvious that the southern Michigan deer are psychologically confined to them just as tightly as their northern brethren.

Movements may occur at any time of the day or night, especially when it's sunny or warm compared with the preceding few days; however, when it's cold, movement and feeding will tend to be concentrated in the warmest part of the day, usually the middle of daylight hours, 9:00 A.M. to 3:00 P.M. Nighttime feeding is common unless it's unusually cold compared with the preceding few days.

In summary, deer are neither metabolically nor physiologically prepared for winter prior to its arrival, and acclimation to winter conditions does not happen overnight. The deer react to early cold with increased activity, which, I believe, is to generate warmth. Once acclimation has occurred and there is snow pack of five inches or more, the deer are confined to using only 5 percent to 10 percent of the land in their habitat, and feeding declines dramatically despite the availability of food. The deer are eager to vacate their winter confinement as soon as weather permits, but if they vacate and the weather worsens, they immediately return.

SPRING

Just as there was no single pattern of behavior and distribution in winter, there is none for spring. If winter breaks early (snow depth is more important in determining this than is temperature alone), the deer immediately become very active and widespread throughout the habitat, using, more than at any other time of year, literally every inch of their territory. Their activity will be spread throughout the twenty-four-hour day, no longer confined to the warmer, less windy times of day.

From late autumn to late winter, it's very unusual to have deer straightline for more than a half mile, but it's not unusual during early spring. When there was enough snow cover, I've tracked deer on many occasions at this time—on several occasions I've tracked deer for a mile or even a mile and a half only to have them turn around and head right back to where they started from. I'm convinced it's a reflection of their curiosity and investigative nature more than anything else. By early spring they've been cooped up in their winter areas for a couple of months, and they're trying as quickly as possible to see what's happened to the rest of their world while they were away.

This period of superactivity lasts approximately two or three weeks and then quickly dies down. As it does so, the larger groupings of deer found in winter begin to splinter as smaller family units go separate ways, and the long-range movements common to very late winter and early spring decrease. When the deer first leave their winter confines, they often return to them for brief periods before venturing farther away for good. During early spring the deer are still extremely active and widespread, despite the decrease in long-range movements and smaller social groupings. Feeding activity increases greatly and tends to disperse the deer because there's no single food source for them to concentrate on.

Spring green-up is not an all-or-nothing phenomenon. Some areas—swamp and pond edges, second-year fallow fields with dark soils, and south-facing slopes—start to green up a week or more before there's even a hint of green-up elsewhere. This is where the deer begin to concentrate, moving off for short periods and coming back.

During this early spring phase, activity begins to decrease, while feeding activity continues to increase. After months of food scarcity, the deer now have concentrated food sources. By the time green-up is widespread (late April in southern Michigan) the winter social groupings have truly splintered, the early spring hyperactivity disappears, and long-range movement has declined. Now activity may occur at any time, most frequently during daylight hours, especially very early and very late in the day.

Once spring green-up occurs, the deer have it pretty easy. There are not yet hoards of stinging, biting insects for them to deal with, it's not yet too hot, water is normally abundant, and high-energy foods are readily available, more so than at any other time of the year. It's the timing that evolution and adaptation have geared the deer towards, for now the demands of the does' pregnancies, the bucks' developing antlers, and the maturational demands of last year's physically developing fawns are all at their peak. Collectively, the deer eat and rest a lot; movement and activity levels are at an annual minimum.

If a late spring winterlike storm hits, the deer react very differently than they would have just a few weeks earlier. They now react as they would in late autumn or early winter, with markedly heightened activity. They do this for the same reason at both times of year: they're cold! In early spring they've lost a good portion of their winter coats since starting to shed them in late February, and their metabolic rates have increased greatly. If they're pregnant does, their metabolic needs are especially high.

Since bucks don't have antlers at this time, it's hard to be certain, but I feel that most lone animals I've seen in spring are bucks. This is confirmed by those instances when I could get a clear look. Contrary to much of the literature, I see no reason to believe that buck groupings have re-formed yet. Personally, I have never seen a bachelor group in southern Michigan in early to midspring.

As leaves begin to unfurl, the deer begin to vacate the open areas. More and more, they move into cover, and when they feed in clover or alfalfa fields, it is only during periods of dim light or at night.

Overall activity drops off dramatically in spring, with two notable exceptions. Last year's fawns, lost and confused because they are on their own for the first time (having been driven off by their dams in mid-May), become hyperactive, as I've described in Chapters 2 and 3. In addition, bucks that are searching for social groupings to lock up with have not yet decreased their activity level.

Beginning about mid-May, therefore, very few deer are seen, except yearlings. Even their sign decreases, and one wonders, "Where have all the deer gone?" At this point the deer are more spread out than at any other time of year.

Each adult doe now has a territory within cover that she will defend, leaving it for only brief periods or not at all.

With regard to buck groups, one often reads that they re-form in spring. This is misleading. In Michigan and other regions with traditional deer management programs, bucks are so heavily harvested that most social groupings are destroyed each year, and surviving bucks must form new groups. By early June adult and yearling bucks have formed bachelor groups, but because food and cover are so readily available, movement in these groups is minimal, too. There is no outside influence—rutting, hunting, poaching—to stimulate activity, so they feed heavily and rest a lot.

By late spring, overall deer activity is at an annual minimum.

SUMMER

What's the single most important event in the annual life cycle of deer? From almost everything you've ever read about deer, you know the answer is the rut, right? Wrong! The purpose of the rut is solely for the propagation of the species through the birth of the fawns each year. If Mother Nature were less consistent in timing the events of late spring and early summer, we'd have no deer at all—and deer would not be the only species wiped out! At the very least, their life cycle would be drastically altered by a different, less predictable, climatic pattern.

In early June 1992, Michigan's U.P. experienced an unusual event. It rained off and on for over a week, and then it froze! Practically the entire fawn crop, dropped just days before, perished. Most of the major events in the life cycles of animals depend on predictable weather patterns; when Mother Nature throws a curve like the one in 1992, the animals pay dearly.

The point is that while the rut may be the most important aspect of deer life for human hunters, for the deer the rut is simply an instinctual process to ensure something of much greater importance: survival of the species.

In Chapter 3, I described the behaviors and distribution of the doe population in some detail, so here I will concentrate on the bucks and yearlings.

Bucks are fickle about their groupings. Rarely, if ever, will two bucks in a bachelor group be closely related by lineage—unlike the doe groups, where maternal instincts, lin-

Born into opulence, this fawn is fortunate. With no unexpected weather calamities and born on time—in fact, early, I took this photo on May 17—she has an excellent chance to reach the minimum of approximately sixty pounds she will need to survive next winter.

eage, and years of association bond them closely. Bucks have no such history, especially in traditional deer management states, where 80 percent to 90 percent of antlered bucks are shot annually.

The result is that bucks come and go from their groups, especially the yearling bucks and especially during the early period of group formation. But because of the gregarious nature of deer and their ties to home areas, and the familiarity that comes with time, buck groups do begin to stabilize somewhat.

In my three years of study I never saw more than two bucks in a group until early summer, so I have no reason to believe that bachelor groups form with any consistency in southern Michigan before that time, and I have seen lone bucks on many occasions, even in late spring (more about these loner bucks later). These observations cause me to wonder if, at least in part, it isn't the disintegration of the doe groups in preparation for birthing that prompts the bucks to then form their bachelor groups.

In any event, it's common in my area by late May/early June to see anywhere from two to seven bucks together. After this time, it is increasingly rare to see loner bucks, with the exception that it is never considered unusual to see a truly exceptional buck by himself. (It is unusual, however, to see a truly exceptional buck in southern Michigan!) Most bucks, then, are associated with other bucks by mid-June.

Michigan researcher John Ozoga strongly believes that buck and doe groups live apart, that they actually occupy different areas within the available range. John is a consummate professional, and if he says that is what the deer do in his area—Michigan's forested U.P.—I fully believe it. But that's not how southern Michigan's agricultural deer behave. Here, it is true there are separate groups of bucks and does, but their ranges overlap, and they frequently feed in an intermingled state.

For two years my wife, Annette, and I took a ride every evening. We traveled the same path each time and always tried to take the drive during the last hour of daylight. From the time does started traveling with their fawns in late June and continuing for the rest of the summer, we often saw buck and doe groups occupying the same areas, feeding side by side and intermingling as they did so.

John Ozoga believes that the reason for the separation he sees is a nutritional-metabolic difference between bucks and does that results in the does getting the nutritionally best range areas. He's probably right. This makes sense for marginal deer habitats, which can offer only a marginal nutritional plane. Southern Michigan deer, however, are usually so well-fed that there'd be no lack for our does and fawns and, therefore, no need for the separation.

Summer is a lazy but important time for the deer. There is normally neither severe drought nor suffocating heat, and except for the minor burdens of lactation on dams and antler development on bucks, there are no significant stressors on the deer. From the time fawns are dropped in early June, the deer don't travel much until the end of August. They have no need to travel; the woods are thick, giving plenty of shade, and food and water are usually plentiful and nearby. Deer frequent swamps, ponds, and other low-lying areas, visiting openings only at night or at both ends of the day, especially in the evening.

Once the panic—and I believe that is the only honest way to describe it—begins to subside in yearlings from their abandonment in mid-May, most bucks join bachelor groups and settle into a calm routine, while the does settle into the margins of the areas claimed by the older does. As the new fawns gain strength and mobility, the yearling doe is allowed to spend more and more time with the dam until finally, by late June, there's no further attempt to keep her away, and doe groups re-form, by lineage, as before.

Late spring and early summer find the deer spread out more evenly across the habitat than at any other time of year. There are no large groupings of deer anywhere. Only yearlings—lost and abandoned and on their own for the first time—have a rough time at this season, and that quickly passes. Deer movement is at a minimum. The only time there's less overall movement is in the dead of winter when there's at least five inches of snow pack and very cold conditions. From June through early September, deer groupings are solidifying, with very high levels of feeding activity, but relatively low overall activity and minimal long-range movements.

AUTUMN

From the time the bucks' antlers harden and they shed their velvet (around September 15 in southern Michigan) and lasting until they've become acclimated to winter conditions (mid-January), they are at their busiest and most active. This time is one of a much easier, more gradual transition for the does; they go gradually from the lazy days of summer to the hectic, disruptive days of the gun season to the hyperactive days of early winter. With the exception of a three- to five-day period of active breeding, the does do not experience the unrelenting activity and stress of the bucks. At this time, on top of everything else, the bucks must deal with being in peril from legitimate hunters and low-life poachers.

It's amazing how well-synchronized a lot of the physiological changes in animals are, year after year. While taking our evening rides in the falls of 1992 and 1993, Annette and I saw an average of five bucks a day during early September. In 1992 we never saw a buck with polished antlers until September 17, but after September 21 we never saw a buck with velvet. In 1993 we saw our first polished antlers on September 15 and never saw a buck with velvet after September 20.

With the shedding of velvet come behavioral changes, too, and while these changes do not occur all at once and may escape detection by the casual observer, they do occur quickly and affect the deer's behavior profoundly.

The first change one sees after shedding is sparring behavior, in which two or more bucks join their antlers and push against one another. During this time one also sees bigger, clearly more dominant bucks executing "threat" behaviors. They approach other bucks with their heads lowered, the hair along their necks raised and their ears flattened along their necks. These "stereotypical displays" send a clear message to subordinate bucks: "Get out of my way!" A very naive yearling might make the mistake of not paying attention once; you can bet he won't make it twice.

These behaviors begin literally hours within the shedding of the velvet and continue, increasing in frequency and intensity, for weeks. In a small percentage of cases (but by no means rare) and always among bucks of near-equal status, these sparring matches do not produce a clear victor, and they'll escalate until true fighting erupts. This is what has happened when you see bucks with broken tines or, in rarer cases, broken main beams. Buck battles can be bloody and to the death

Fights occur with increasing frequency in the later pre-rut period and are most often between bucks that were previously unknown to one another. Only when sparring and stereotypical posturing do not settle the dominance issue will a fight take place. I do not know and have never read an estimate of the number of sparring matches a small buck (four-, six-, or eight-points, for example) has each fall, but I'm cer-

A young buck like this in a well-balanced herd will very quickly learn his place; during the frenzied period of the rut, he'll maintain his distance from more dominant bucks, and avoid unnecessary confrontations.

tain that it's in the hundreds for each buck because if before mid-October you watch two, three, or four polished-antlered bucks even for just a few minutes, you are almost guaranteed to see a sparring match or stereotypical posturing.

During this time does and fawns will be actively feeding, and while the bucks feed, too, it's increasingly clear as autumn progresses that feeding is of secondary importance to the bucks. Their primary focus is on settling the issue of dominance. And make no mistake about it, dominance at this time is not about food supply or who will lead the herd, it is about breeding rights. Period.

As the issue of dominance begins to sort itself out, the bucks drift apart. It's clear they're intolerant of each other. They become loners for the most part, and by early October (at least, in my area) buck groups no longer exist.

A lot of white-tailed deer activity takes place at night; nocturnal patterns are less common only in the dead of winter. Some research biologists believe that as much as 90 percent of all breeding, for example, takes place under cover of darkness. I've observed in southern Michigan that bucks simply disappear from view entirely starting from almost the very moment they polish their antlers. Such a transition could not be natural! I am inclined to attribute it to the prevalence of poaching (see previous chapter).

Every single year without fail I hear shooting at night from about the first week in September until around New Year's. In a typical year, I hear night shots six or eight times during those months. When you consider that I work midnights (so I'm seldom home for most of the night) and that when I am home I might not hear shots because I'm asleep or the TV is on too loud, and when you add that most poaching is probably done during the day when no one would give a second thought to shots, you begin to appreciate the magnitude of poaching!

Those in the DNR who say that poaching is not a major problem have their heads in the sand. Next to habitat destruction, I'm convinced that poaching is the most serious threat to wildlife. In the area of my study, poaching claims more deer per year than legal hunting does, and I don't believe my area is different in this regard from any other area. Many in the Michigan DNR try to say that the nocturnal shift in buck behavior at this time of the year is natural. I say that's absurd! I spend a lot of time photographing deer. I photographed much more in 1994 than usual and, during June, July and August, I averaged seeing fifteen deer per day, of which four were bucks. By the first week of September, those numbers were down to three deer per day and 0.3 bucks! After September 11, I didn't even see a buck in ten days of trying. In disgust I gave up and began photographing in southern Ontario, Canada. From September 17 until November 12, in more than seventeen days of photography, I averaged seeing more than thirty deer per day and seven bucks! The total and complete disappearance of southern Michigan's deer, and especially her bucks in autumn, is not natural!

In any event, there's a very remarkable change in the bucks' behavior in September. The animals I've watched day in and day out all summer suddenly disappear by the third week of September. Doe numbers decline, too, but not as "miraculously" as the bucks, and even naive yearlings become nocturnal at this time. This change is all the more dramatic when you realize that at this very same time, the bucks' activity levels are increasing considerably; the prerut period is like an itch the bucks can't scratch, and it drives them crazy.

There are several activities bucks engage in during the autumn, all of them geared toward the one, overriding goal: breeding.

Sparring

It's often written that all deer are interested in the outcomes of sparring matches. Don't believe it. I've watched more than three hundred sparring contests, and the does and fawns that were nearby, while perhaps tossing an initial glance in the direction of the sparring, have never shown any additional response. Bucks, however, are very interested and may even become active participants. If bigger bucks are present, they'll either completely ignore the smaller bucks that are sparring, begin a sparring match themselves—or one of them may well rush in and separate the initial combatants, thereby asserting his dominance over all the bucks in attendance.

Rubbing

Rubs are small areas of intentional damage by a deer to a tree or bush. They serve as signposts made by bucks to get the attention of other deer. We're quite sure of a couple of the functions of rubs, even though we're not certain of the precise mechanisms involved. They help bucks strengthen their neck muscles, much as sparring matches do. Later (and probably most important), they somehow serve to identify the individual that made them.

Recent research by Grant Woods of Clemson University adds greatly to our understanding of rubs. Rubs are not only visual signposts, but also olfactory messages that identify which animals have worked them. All deer are interested in buck rubs, not just bucks; does will, at least on occasion, rub on them, too, apparently to let the bucks know their state of breeding readiness.

This is probably the most unusual rub I have ever found. It's on a lower limb of a giant oak tree. The tree grows part way down a rather steep hillside; the limb clears the hill's crest by roughly two feet and runs parallel with the ground at that point. I cannot recall ever seeing another horizontal buck rub, nor a buck rub that strictly involved just a single limb of a tree.

Movements

At the same time the bucks begin working rubs in earnest they also expand their range considerably. Research to date does not agree on how much the range increases or for which bucks it increases the most—all bucks? only the bigger ones?

My own observations do not answer these questions, either. All I can say is that the bucks' range increases significantly. At this point (October 10–15 in southern Michigan) bucks begin to feed less and move more. They're basically alone, and when they run into each other, they're much more aggressive.

Scrapes

Like rubs, scrapes serve as both visual and olfactory signposts. Scrapes show up after the creation of rubs begins to slow down, usually around October 25 in southern Michigan. Scrapes are almost always near an overhanging limb, which the deer chews on and rubs the forehead on. Generally scrapes are found in association with other scrapes, forming what is called a "scrape line," containing anywhere from three to ten or more scrapes over a line between three hundred yards and one-half mile long. Scrape lines are usually found along the edge of a cover, a prominent contour line within cover, or along some form such as a fenceline.

In my study, about 30 percent of the scrapes were reworked and/or revisited by other bucks, does, or fawns over a period of two to three weeks. Bucks often rub their antlers through the scrape. A buck, a doe, or a fawn frequently leaves a footprint in a scrape and defecates (25 percent of the time) and/or urinates on it.

Research has not solved all the mysteries surrounding scrapes. It is believed that most scrape visits occur at night, and my own observations bear this out. I've only once seen a buck at a scrape during daylight, and he totally ignored it! He neither lowered his head to the scrape nor paid attention to the overhanging limb; he simply stopped for a moment, then slowly walked on.

Young bucks fortunate enough to be members of well-balanced herds are little affected by the rut. Researchers at the University of Georgia, who've studied chemical communications extensively, believe that one of the functions of dominant bucks' scent-marking behaviors is to suppress breeding desires in younger bucks. I photograph extensively in the autumn and, based upon my observations, believe that this is true, or at least that young bucks in well-balanced herds are less agitated and active than those in badly skewed herds. The better balanced the herd, the more young bucks seem to concentrate on feeding, resting and, in general, staying out of harm's way. Clearly it is not nature's desire to have young bucks actively involved in breeding. If things progress more naturally—meaning through a well-balanced herd structure—then they are not involved.

Once does start cycling in and breeding begins, the creation and refreshening of scrapes ends abruptly. Interest in the scrapes reappears briefly about thirty days later, as some does and six-month-old fawns cycle in, but this is minimal and lasts only a few days.

Breeding

While the bucks have been expending huge amounts of energy on the settling of dominance ranking and later sign-making behaviors, does and fawns having been living their lives in a continuation of summer's leisurely ways. They're still grouped as earlier and feeding heavily. Except for the

A typical or classic scrape. Note the clearing of all duff from the soil and the overhead limb. Scent markings will be left both on the ground and on the limb.

forty-eight hours before each doe cycles into estrus, her activity level does not increase. Of course, since food sources have dwindled and changed, long-distance travel usually increases for the does and fawns too, but their overall activity level changes little.

Research shows that roughly forty-eight hours prior to estrus, a doe leaves her family unit to actively search for a buck, most likely a specific buck of her choice. Her heightened activity, however, will be within the confines of her normal range. At this time, her activity level may increase twentyfold or more. This is an important point to understand; the doe, while increasing her activity level markedly, does so *only* within her normal range. Bucks, especially dominant bucks, increase not only their activity levels but also greatly expand their normal range. Once she finds that buck (or a substitute) she stays with him until she cycles in and is bred repeatedly to ensure conception. She is fertile for twenty-four to thirty hours. Then when she cycles out, she returns to her family unit and resumes her normal daily routine.

The disruption of her life for breeding lasts about three days altogether, whereas the breeding-related activities for the buck last approximately two months!

During this feverish period of activity, the bucks are also being heavily poached and legally hunted. The result is that the bucks are superactive—but also very cautious. They stick to cover like glue. They're active mostly in low-light periods of the day and at night. Wherever they're heavily hunted, it's only within very heavy cover that they will move about during broad daylight. Then, just before the actual breeding phase of the rut (November 18–25 in southern Michigan), they abandon their solitary ways and can be found near areas of doe activity. This is the time when hunters can catch bucks doing truly stupid things they normally wouldn't do—such as being out in the open during broad daylight.

Hunting pressure affects the behavior of doe groups, but less drastically and more gradually. At least in my area, poaching is done to procure antlers, seldom, if ever, for meat. For bucks, therefore, the choice is to become noc-

turnal—almost overnight—or die. As more people appear—
farmers bringing in their crops, poachers, archers, and preseason gun hunters scouting the region—does become more
and more cautious (stopping longer just inside cover, running immediately at the first hint of danger) and more nocturnal. Also, their feeding areas change, depending on the
harvesting of crops and abundance or absence of mast in a
given year. Certainly the does and fawns will not be feeding
at the same times and in the same places in November that
they were in late September.

Once the rut is past (late November) and most hunters
have left the woods (end of November), the deer quickly
change again. After the bucks' frantic activity level, they're
physically spent and initially all they want to do is rest.
After a week or so, they begin to feed more. In open areas,
feeding remains nocturnal; daylight feeding is done within
cover. Does give up nocturnal ways much more quickly than
bucks and revert to daytime activity within days of the
hunters vacating the woods.

This pattern of increased feeding but decreased overall
activity among bucks and sustained feeding with gradually
increased activity levels among does continues until the
early winter acclimation period, and the seasonal cycle
repeats.

14

Feeding Habits
Throughout the Year

According to the *Encyclopedia Britannica*, "Certain herbivores are monophagous (restricted to one type of food), as is the koala to eucalyptus, but most have at least a moderate variety in their diets." Reading that tickled me. Biologists believe that the whitetail (*Odocoileus virginianus*) has a more varied diet than any other herbivore. More than six hundred species of vegetation are known to be consumed by whitetails. I knew from the start that I wouldn't be able to catalog everything the deer ate in my study area; that task would be herculean. But I did have three goals concerning feeding: (1) discover the most common foods eaten, (2) determine when they are eaten on an annual basis, and (3) chronicle variations of feeding behavior throughout the year.

I knew it would take a tremendous amount of time and rigorous discipline to accomplish even these modest goals. To help ensure my success, I stuck religiously to the following routine:

- With very few exceptions, I was in the field every day

- Each day in the field I assayed at least one type of habitat (a crop field or hardwood woodlot, for example), attentive to any sign of feeding
- I recorded daily in minute detail all findings, as well as my thoughts and impressions
- I tried to identify all species of vegetation the deer were feeding on—provided I was certain that deer were doing the feeding

WINTER

Just as with the distribution and movement of deer in winter, their feeding patterns are also very dependent on weather conditions. Particularly important are depth of snow pack (if any), the length of time into the winter period, and temperature, especially windchill temperature. Also important in my study area is the presence or absence of both standing corn and mast.

A couple of decades ago it was common, even in scientific journals, to read that deer were "browsers" as compared with "grazers," but now it's widely recognized that this is highly variable, depending on location. Beyond a doubt, the deer of Maine or much of Michigan's U.P.—or any other heavily forested region—will procure a much higher percentage of their dietary intake by browsing than will the deer of agricultural areas.

In areas like southern Michigan, agricultural crops, as well as forbs, fruits, and mast (hard mast such as acorns), form a higher percentage of the deer intake.

Beyond question, if there's less than five inches of snow pack (or none at all), crops and mast (if present) are the most frequent form of intake for deer in my area—I would have to say at least 75 percent. Soft mast, in the form of fruits, and forbs make up practically all the rest.

Of course, this figure I'm using of five inches is arbitrary. Some researchers have said three inches is the critical depth. The important thing to understand is that the deer are pretty easily influenced by snow cover; they will not dig very deeply to get at herbaceous growth. So if there's snow pack over five inches, reliance on crop fields and ground-hugging herbaceous growth falls off substantially.

Even then, however, if there's standing corn, it will be a prime target for every deer in the area. In the winter of 1992–93, because of an unusually wet autumn, all local cornfields were left standing, and I assayed them on three separate occasions: the first two weeks of December, the end of January, and the end of March.

As one would have predicted, only about 10 percent of the corncobs showed signs of damage in December (cobs are usually the only part of the corn plant the deer consume after the plants wither in the autumn). By the first of February, 30 percent showed damage, and in March some of the fields showed 100 percent damage, and others 50 percent to 60 percent. It must be noted that as winter progresses it becomes increasingly difficult to tell whether the corn damage is from deer, squirrels, or raccoons. Furthermore, I am convinced that once a corncob is fed upon by any animal (deer, squirrel, or raccoon), it is much more likely to be fed upon again by the same animal or another until it is consumed entirely.

Feeding damage by deer varies with the season, with the density of deer, and the severity of winter's weather. In autumn or winter's uncut cornfields, the damage is done only to the cobs; the longer they remain, the more extensive the damage.

Such crop damage shows additional distinct patterns worth noting. The smaller the field, the more heavily damaged it will be. The perimeters of all fields are always hit hardest. Sections of fields that are secluded or sheltered from humans are consistently favored. When snow pack is shallow or nonexistent, all of these factors apply equally to clover and alfalfa fields, too.

As winter progresses, there are marked feeding changes. Although gradual, feeding changes are invariably heralded by deterioration in weather conditions. Early in the winter, increased snow depth is the most frequent form of deteriorating weather; from late January on, low temperatures and/or increased winds are more likely to be the factors that bring on changes. The changes are a lessened dependence on crops and an increase in browsing activity.

Throughout the year whenever there's leaf growth, you can see signs of deer browsing on them, but in my area there are no signs of woody plant damage at all until mid-January. Woody growth browsing then increases until green-up in the spring. I found the most heavily browsed species to include:

white pine	sumac
white cedar (very few in my area)	sassafras
red cedar	white spruce
apple	eastern poplar
red maple	oak (saplings only)
Canadian plum	common juniper
silky dogwood	basswood (saplings only)
gray dogwood	rock elm
red osier dogwood	thornapple
silver maple	briers
willow	red pine

By the end of January feeding becomes confined pretty much to the warmer periods of the day, whether that is nighttime or daytime, and by the second half of winter almost all feeding will be confined to cover or the very edges of cover. These changes are even more marked if there's snow pack over five inches. All feeding activity, regardless of snow pack, temperature, and windchill, is greatly reduced—as much as 40 percent—from the midwinter period until spring green-up.

We read frequently that, as ruminants, white-tailed deer are able to consume large amounts of food quickly and then retreat to secure areas to begin at leisure the process of regurgitation, cud chewing, and final digestion. While this is certainly possible, when it's meant to imply that such behavior is typical or commonplace, it's misleading. It is by no means typical or commonplace. On many, many occasions, I've watched deer feed in a very leisurely, relaxed manner.

On one bitterly cold, sunny day in February 1991, I saw a deer slowly working its way down a thin fenceline separating two very large fallow fields. I stopped to observe with my binoculars. The deer worked its way along the fenceline until it came to a south-facing slope where there was an area I later measured to be eighteen feet by fourteen feet, devoid of snow. It was 3:50 P.M. when the deer entered the snow-free area and began to feed. I watched for fifty-seven minutes until I was too bored and cold to watch any more. During that whole time the deer fed almost continuously, never wandering more than twenty feet in any direction. Finally, as I moved, I spooked the deer, and it ran away.

In December 1992, while assaying an uncut cornfield at 2:00 P.M., I discovered three deer, a doe and two fawns, feeding in the corn. I watched for more than an hour as they slowly fed away from me. I could give countless such examples. Clearly, it's wrong to believe that deer commonly gulp their food and seek shelter. In my observations, leisurely feeding is the rule rather than the exception at all times of year.

SPRING

Changes in feeding behavior of the deer do not, of course, coincide with our calendar, but rather with weather changes we connect with our calendar. Increasing sunlight, warmer days and nights, the diminishing and disappearance of snow pack, and the beginning of green-up are the signs that herald feeding changes. And, unlike the gradual behavioral changes of winter deer, changes in spring can occur very quickly—sometimes literally overnight.

Once snow pack diminishes to the point that there are areas that are 15 percent to 20 percent snow-free, the deer abandon their winter feeding behavior. They no longer browse, no longer confine feeding to cover or the edges of cover. Now they concentrate instead on areas associated with new growth—pond/swamp edges, fallow fields with dark soils, hardwood woodlots with little or no undergrowth, and southerly and westerly facing slopes (where the sun has the greatest impact early).

Changes in feeding behaviors parallel very closely the changes in movement and distribution that were described in Chapter 13. When the deer first change their feeding behavior, they simultaneously go from the period of least movement and largest concentrations to a period of very exaggerated movement with smaller groupings. As spring progresses, movements diminish (especially long-distance movements) and the groupings cleave more and more. Within two weeks most of the deer are spending a majority of their time in the area(s) where they are feeding while the groupings are becoming smaller, female-dominated, family groups (as opposed to the larger, aggregate groups of winter).

During this same two-week period, spring green-up is spreading quickly, and so are the deer. By mid-April they are no longer confined to feeding during the warmer portions of the day, and nocturnal feeding becomes common. Herbaceous growth forms the mainstay of their diet. Browsing activity is abandoned almost entirely.

This is a time of heavy feeding. The deer revert quickly from their starvation diet of winter to gluttonous gorging.

During the past three years, I've observed deer eating the following items during this very early spring period: clover, alfalfa, trout lilies (roots only), cattails (all parts of visible shoots), swamp grasses (leaves only), spring beauties (roots only), snake grass (ends of shoots), moss of various kinds (upper portions and, on occasion, beneath the soil), and an old decaying stump. (In addition to shredding and eating the stump, it appeared the deer ate some soil, too.)

This list highlights a major weakness of mine: I couldn't identify some of the items I saw the deer consume. For example, I have labeled as "swamp grass" the several varieties of grass and grasslike plants found growing along the edges of swamps and ponds from damp soil locations to water depths of four or five inches. The main point, however, is that during this early spring period, the deer are not very choosy—anything that is green or shows signs of life will be investigated and probably consumed by the deer. Spring also brings behaviors not routinely observed at other times of year.

Much more frequently, the deer will dig or root for food; for example, trout lily and spring beauty roots. Also, on two separate occasions, I've found old decaying stumps the deer have torn up and partially eaten, along with some of the surrounding soils. I've read that deer and other animals eat soil to obtain needed minerals, but I've only witnessed this personally during early spring. As an aside, one of the best places in the world to observe moose is Algonquin Park, in Ontario, Canada. From late April, through much of July, moose are commonly seen right along the roadway as they seek salt concentrations left over from winter clearing operations. Biologists believe that because of their winter diets, by spring each year the moose are starved for minerals and it's this nutritional need that brings them roadside. I suspect it's a similar mineral deficiency that causes the white-tail to root in the spring.

Once green-up is under way, the deer find they have an abundance of items to choose from, as the flora goes from being withered and brown to green and vital. Within two weeks, nature has provided the deer with a smorgasbord, and they become quite selective about feeding, as they always are when given the opportunity. At this time they feed very heavily any time of the day, and I've often seen them feeding right out in the open.

The items I've seen deer consume once green-up is widespread are trout lilies (entire plant, flowers, leaves, and roots), spring beauties (entire plant, including roots), red trillium (leaves only), white trillium (leaves and flowers), snake grass, skunk cabbage (end section of leaves only), wild ginger (leaves and stems), smooth Solomon's-seal (end section of leaves only), duckweed, arrowhead, clover, alfalfa, and corn plants. In late spring, when corn plants are four to twelve inches tall, deer can do a lot of damage. They'll eat the entire plants and trample them, doing serious damage to the corn crop.

Tree leaves that I've seen the deer eat at this time include red maple, slippery elm, rock elm, oak, basswood, and sassafras.

I'm certain this list does not accurately convey the enormous variety of the deer menu, much greater (especial-

Freshly unfurled leaves are extremely high in protein content and actively sought.

ly in the second half of the spring period) than at any other time of year.

SUMMER

I think of summer as beginning in the middle of May or at least in the third week of May, because until this time, the spring period is essentially unchanged for the deer. Once the does separate themselves to drop their new fawns, their patterns and feeding habits stay pretty much the same until the newly arrived fawns are capable of traveling and feeding with them, beginning about the first of July.

While winter damage to corn is to the corncobs only, damage in the summer is to the leaves only. The deer also utilize the summer corn for shade and cover.

As described earlier, the does become territorial during their birthing period, and for roughly six weeks they live in virtual solitude with their fawns. During this time, they seldom wander outside of a two- to four-acre area, and all available vegetation will be at least sampled. Newly unfurled leaves, however, form the staple of their diet, with crops (clover, alfalfa, and corn), wildflowers, and forbs comprising the remainder.

During this period, I've seen deer consume:

smooth Solomon's-seal
duckweed
arrowhead
corn (leaves and stalks)
mustard (terminal portions only)
oats
barley
clover
alfalfa
tree leaves (red maple, slippery elm, rock elm,
            sassafras, and basswood)

While the does are in their territorial phase, the bucks, re-forming their bachelor groups, live mainly around the perimeters of these areas, especially near water and heavily shaded cover. Ponds, swamps, and isolated lake shores become the bucks' hang-outs. There, they consume large quantities of aquatic plants (very high in mineral content), wildflowers, forbs, and crops. Within cover, feeding can occur at any time, but crop forays are nocturnal or at least crepuscular. Once they move into the crops, bucks will often spend their whole nights feeding and bedding intermittently until dawn, when they again seek shelter.

For bucks, this pattern stays pretty much the same until their antlers harden in mid-September. The does and their month-old fawns show a similar pattern beginning around the first of July. The perimeters of the crop fields always sustain the heaviest damage.

I've read that deer don't like corn from the time it's knee high until it tassels out, because it's bitter tasting at

Both bucks and does require a good deal of moisture. How much is dependent upon the foods they're eating, physiological stresses each is under, and temperature. Averages probably run between one and two quarts per day. Lactating does require more.

that time. I can't say if it's bitter, but I have observed that
the deer eat it far less during that time and that what little
they do eat is the ends of the leaves.

The fawns are growing rapidly during this period. They
nearly triple their birth weight by July first, going from
roughly seven pounds to twenty-plus; then they nearly
quadruple their birth weight by September. By July, the
fawns mimic their dams' feeding behaviors, while weaning is
gradually taking place. Though some fawns are still nursing
into August, by mid-July most are functioning ruminants,
and the bulk of their intake is the vegetation they consume.
Feeding is learned behavior, based on observing the deer
they're with, and a little experimentation on their own.

AUTUMN

In most areas south of the historical boreal forest line,
autumn is the most tumultuous time for deer. To a very
large degree, hunters and recreational hunting have
replaced nature's far harsher methods of dealing with
excess numbers. As much as 30 percent of our overall deer
herds are culled annually in some areas, at least 20 percent
in most locations. As many as 90 percent of legally antlered
bucks may fall to hunters annually. All this pressure makes
a dramatic impact on deer behaviors. Early season archery
hunters—and poachers!—impact the deer early; by late
September, a lot of deer are already in a nocturnal mode of
survival.

At first, their diet does not change much: mast (princi-
pally acorns, if present), crops, soft mast (fruits and
berries), and forbs. But *when* these items are consumed
changes; feeding becomes nocturnal suddenly for bucks,
more gradually for does and fawns.

During our evening drive in the autumn of 1992,
Annette and I were seeing an average of 3.1 bucks per day
until September 28, when that figure suddenly plummeted.
We didn't see another buck until October 18, and then not
another until December 21! In 1993, we were seeing an
average of 5.4 bucks per day, but that figure dropped to 1.3
through October. Then on November 3, we stopped seeing

any bucks until December 22. Numbers of deer other than bucks also dropped significantly, as more and more of them sought the safety of shelter during all daylight hours.

During October (especially late October for does and fawns) crops continue to be the mainstay of their diet. Alfalfa, soybeans, clover, and corn (cobs only now) are the most frequent. Acorns play an interesting role in the feeding behavior of deer.

In the autumn of 1991 my area of southern Michigan had the largest acorn crop in my memory. Consequently, the deer stayed in or near the widely scattered hardwood wood-lots throughout the entire autumn, and the deer were seen in groups of three to ten, or even more. In both 1992 and 1993, however, we experienced a total failure of the acorn crop. In these years the deer were very widespread, group-ings were much smaller on the average, and we saw no areas of heavy concentration of deer.

I've read several times (usually writers in the South) that large mast crops make hunting difficult because the deer tend to scatter. I can understand that in areas with widespread mast-bearing trees. In southeastern Michigan, however, we have little mast other than from oaks, and our oaks tend to be concentrated in relatively small monoga-mous stands. If they don't produce, we have no other single food source to concentrate the deer, and hunting becomes much more difficult.

I honestly believe the single most reliable predictor of overall hunting success in southeastern Michigan is the preseason presence or absence of acorns. Another important determinant is whether farmers get in their corn crop prior to the gun season. Hunting in an area with lots of standing corn is tough. It happens often here.

Another thing I've read (always in the popular press) is that deer have a strong fondness for mushrooms and that mushrooms, on occasion, serve to concentrate them. Like the situation with acorns, perhaps that's true in some areas, but I've seen nothing that leads me to believe it's true for my area. I've seen no sign of deer consuming large quan-tities of mushrooms. Instead, I've seen deer here ignore mushrooms entirely. On countless occasions, I've watched

Mushrooms are a favorite whitetail food in many regions. They are not a favorite, and in fact are almost completely ignored, throughout southern Michigan. The reason lies in why deer go after mushrooms to begin with. Mushrooms are very high in certain minerals, especially nitrogen and phosphorous. Deer deficient in these minerals will thus consume mushrooms. Agricultural areas, such as southern Michigan, experience so much fertilization of their soils with nitrogen- and phosphorous-based fertilizers that the deer are never deficient in these minerals (unless ill or diseased). As a general rule: loam and clay soils are higher in mineral content than are sandy soils; and agricultural lands, golf courses, and fertilized lawns or gardens are very high in mineral content. Hence deer will not often seek mushrooms in these areas. Aquatic vegetation is also very high in mineral content, and is heavily consumed, especially in spring and early summer; thus, if aquatics are readily available the deer may opt for them in preference to mushrooms. Forested regions are, in general, lower in their mineral content than open areas.

many types of mushroom stands bloom, grow, and wither without being eaten by any animals other than squirrels and an occasional bird.

Bucks lose interest in feeding beginning in mid-October as their activity level picks up. They rub, spar, posture, and chase does. From the hunter's point of view, the problem is that they do these things mostly under the cover of darkness. When they feed—acorns, crops, fruits (apples, plums, wild grapes), and forbs—they do that at night, too. From the first or second week in November until the end of November, they feed very little and run often. Bucks, especially bigger bucks, are frequently in the company of a single doe, and they'll often make mistakes at this time, which make them vulnerable to hunters. This is a hunter's best chance of catching a buck doing something foolish, but even at this time, one's best chance is in thick cover—bucks may do foolish things, but they're not stupid!

By the end of November, older bucks are ready to feed again (and younger bucks ready to feed more). They'll isolate themselves (alone, not with other bucks), rest a lot, and gradually begin feeding more heavily. Acorns, crops, fruits, and forbs make up their diet. They maintain their nocturnal patterns for the most part. Younger bucks may fall in with a female family unit or they may hang out alone. If with a group, they'll be more active, in more open areas, during late evening and early daylight hours.

Does and fawns, despite not having nearly the same pressure as bucks, nonetheless gradually revert to cover and nocturnal habits during and immediately following the gun season. However, they'll quickly resume their normal end-of-the-day feeding routines once the pressure eases.

15

Deer Sign, Part I
Rubs and Scrapes

Any serious deer hunter or naturalist who wants to decipher whitetail breeding behavior must understand rubs and scrapes. Rubs appear first, scrapes a month or five weeks later. For years I suspected what I was able to confirm with three years of field study: there are great variations in the frequency, intensity, meaning, visitation rates, and reworking or refreshening of rubs and scrapes. Biologists say this variation depends on at least five factors: buck:doe ratio, deer density, age-class structure of the herd (particularly the buck segment), nutritional plane, and length of the breeding season (mainly latitude dependent).

In the case of rubs, these factors translate into differences in the time span over which rubs are made, the number of rubs created, and the size of the trees rubbed. With scrapes, the differences are found in time span, frequency, size, and frequency of visitation and reworking.

For years I've read stories of hunters having great success by identifying and hunting over scrape lines and rub lines. For just as many years, I've been puzzled over why my personal experiences in Michigan didn't correspond with what I'd read. Michigan bucks, it seemed, didn't habitually rework scrapes as the articles led me to expect. I've been fortunate enough over the years to travel, observe, photograph, and hunt deer in a wide variety of places. What I've learned is that Michigan bucks are not different from bucks in other places, but their herd structure is radically different, and this produces markedly different behaviors.

As I have said earlier, when breeding competition is minimized (as it is in Michigan), one result is that breeding-related behaviors vary erratically and are not as predictable. Until we balance our herds, obtaining near equal (at least 1:3 or better) ratios of bucks to does, hunters in Michigan will never know the thrill of truly patterning a buck. And in my opinion there's no greater thrill in hunting. When you are able to successfully hunt or photograph a buck because you could predict his behavior, you never forget the experience! This is rarely possible in Michigan.

Remember the purported function of rubs and scrapes is that of a visual and olfactory "signpost" to identify their maker to other deer.

RUBS

Bucks make rubs by rubbing their antlers on the trunk and limbs until they remove bark. The forcefulness of the process varies over time; in general, rubs show increased force and destructiveness as we get deeper into the various phases of the prerut. Early rubs (early September to early October) show little damage. They're usually on bushes and smaller trees (diameters of a half to one and a half inches). These rubs may involve broken limbs, but the tree trunk or main stem of the bush is not usually broken. During this time, rubbing frequency is low; rubs are few and far between.

As the season progresses, rubs begin to show marked changes. Beginning in early October, rubs appear on somewhat larger bushes and trees and generally show heavier, more extensive damage. The length and percentage of girth both become greater, as well as the percentage of xylem (sapwood layer) exposed. At this phase, it's common for trees to be broken, and the frequency of rubbing increases.

During the chase phase of the rut (end of October to the third week of November in southern Michigan), there's a noticeable increase in the amount of damage the bucks inflict on their rubs. The size of tree increases slightly, and the average length and girth of the rub rises, as well as the percentage of xylem exposed. These rubs often break the tree or bush completely. Rubbing frequency is at a peak; a buck may make as many as fifteen rubs per day now, perhaps even more.

Once the actual breeding phase of the rut begins, both rubbing frequency and average tree size decrease, and also overall destructiveness.

Biologists theorize that the slow start to signpost creation reflects the time lag between onset of hormonal changes and the appearance of behavioral changes. The breeding cycle is an elaborate stimulus-response process, one which is not brought about overnight. Certain "triggering" events must take place before the deer are ready, both physiologically and psychologically.

As desire builds in the more dominant bucks, they become increasingly frustrated; they are ready, but no does are yet willing to "stand" for them. They take out their frustration on bucks of lesser dominance and by making rubs. Of course, the younger bucks are frustrated, too; not only are they beginning to feel the same sexual frustration as the more dominant bucks, but also they're being bullied by them!

SCRAPES

Scrapes follow essentially the same serial changes as rubs, but their appearance emerges roughly three weeks later, and there are many fewer of them in total. Created by a buck pawing away the litter of leaves, grass, and duff to expose the soil, scrapes vary greatly in size and in thoroughness of preparation. Early scrapes are so incomplete that they may be easily overlooked. The first ones may be a foot or a foot and a half long and half as wide, with leaves and grass left in them. Later, there are more scrapes, and they take on a more classic appearance: about two feet by two feet in size and cleaned out down to the soil with one or more hoof prints in them. They often smell of urine because the buck has urinated ("rub-urinated") on them. One of the world's foremost authorities on olfactory communication in whitetails is Karl Miller, from the University of Georgia. Dr. Miller states emphatically that the tarsal gland is the most important gland in whitetail olfactory communication. Bucks will stand over a scrape they've created, or a scrape they are checking, and hold their hind legs in such a manner that the tarsal glands, located on the inner side of the hocks, are in contact; they'll then urinate in such a manner that the urine dribbles down their legs and across the glands. They'll rub their legs together at the same time, thus mixing the urine and the glandular secretions, which then run onto the scrape. In this way the buck leaves his "signature" on the scrape. (Does rub-urinate as well, and they also do so on scrapes. Additionally, both bucks and does will rub-urinate at any time of the year when they want to leave their signature for any reason.) Often, they'll leave droppings on them, too, and during this phase of the prerut most scrapes, and all "primary" scrapes, will have the characteristic overhanging branch from a nearby tree.

It's believed that other deer—bucks and does—can identify the scrape's maker by the various odors he deposits. In 1982, Atkeson and Marchinton identified glands on the foreheads of deer that become more active during the breeding season. Bucks, and less often does, rub these glands across the terminal portions of the overhanging branch, thereby leaving their scent. They also chew on them and rub their nares (nasal openings) on them. It is believed that these various body substances left by the deer add up to an olfactory "calling card" that can be identified by any other deer that checks the scrape.

Heightened scraping activity lasts about two weeks, and then rapidly decreases, ending almost entirely by the end of November.

My observations in southern Michigan differ from those of some others around the country, and this is because of differences I mentioned earlier: ratios of bucks to does, deer densities, age-class structure of the herd (particularly the buck segment), and length of the breeding season.

As far as we know, the function of rubs and scrapes is to identify the sign maker to others in the herd, letting other bucks know the maker is a force to be reckoned with and letting does know that he's available. What this boils down to is a form of advertising. We know from the business world that advertising is essential in a competitive market. Where there's little or no competition, there's no point in advertising. This is why sign making decreases wherever you have a markedly skewed buck:doe ratio, as in Michigan. There are only a few bucks to service the needs of all the does, so they don't need to advertise their availability.

Why, under these circumstances, doesn't sign making disappear altogether? In many places it very nearly does; however, sign making is an innate behavior (as opposed to learned), so it does not die out entirely. Some minimal amount of rubbing and scraping activity will always be present, no matter how few bucks an area has.

To be successful, breeding behaviors must be synchronized within the herd. As I've mentioned earlier, biologists refer to a window of opportunity for the survival of fawns, particularly in the northmost parts of the deer's range— even the northmost parts of southern Michigan. Some researchers believe that the bucks regulate this synchronicity through the production of pheromones, chemicals which, when detected by the does, stimulate their sexual responsiveness. Does produce pheromones, too, and these also help to coordinate both their and the bucks' state of readiness.

As deer densities increase, this synchronization also increases because the deer have closer and more continuous contact with each other. There may be additional factors besides pheromones that regulate this synchronization, factors which research has not yet identified. If this theory is correct, we would expect more sign making where deer densities are higher, unless it is canceled out by the effects of other factors, such as lopsided ratios of bucks:does or age-class structures skewed to younger bucks.

Researchers (Ozoga and Verme in Michigan, Marchinton et al. in Georgia, and others) believe sign making is much more common in older bucks than in yearlings, and they also believe the character of the sign changes with maturity. When the age-class structure favors older animals, scrapes and rubs become larger, more frequent, and are made on larger trees. If a herd is skewed toward younger animals, overall sign making decreases.

This was one of the largest white-tailed bucks I have ever seen. I'd "guesstimate" his weight at 230 to 250 pounds! As I sat in a blind watching him for more than an hour, he was never more than perhaps fifty yards from me and he scent marked almost continuously! He went from one bush and tree limb to another, thrashing each soundly, and he created two scrapes. The entire time his ears were laid back along his neck line, the hair along the nape of the neck was elevated, and he walked in a very stiff-legged gait. All signs of dominance. It's quite easy to understand, when you witness such behaviors, just how it is that a buck's neck girth can expand so dramatically in such a rapid manner. The sudden increase in hormone levels in autumn in combination with the tremendous workout that dominant bucks give the neck muscles can induce a doubling of girth in just a couple of days! Immature—non-dominant—bucks can never attain these neck-girth dimensions.

Everything associated with breeding is heightened when the nutritional plane is elevated. Embryo-per-doe rates are higher, recruitment rates are higher, and frequency of rubs and scrapes is higher. Birth ratios of bucks and does is altered too. This only stands to reason. Nature puts a check on deer populations when necessary and, conversely, increases the population when the habitat can sustain it because of extra available resources.

Researchers at the University of Georgia have captured pregnant does and estimated conception dates by a process called "backdating." They've found a nine-week breeding period that peaks the first week in November, and they've determined that rubbing begins approximately eight weeks prior to the breeding peak, increases gradually in frequency until two weeks after the breeding peak, and then diminishes rapidly thereafter. By a month after breeding peak, rubbing has all but stopped.

This same research has found that scrapes begin to appear in low frequency roughly eight weeks prior to peak breeding, increasing very rapidly three weeks before peak breeding, maintaining that level for about four weeks (including the actual week of peak breeding), and declining rapidly over the following three weeks. By about five weeks later, scraping has died out entirely (Litchfield 1987).

The Michigan DNR believes the peak breeding period in southern Michigan is November 16–24, and my observations of rubbing and scraping fit well with the Georgia findings; however, Michigan's actual breeding period is believed to last only two weeks (remember the window of opportunity?). Here, therefore, rubs first appear about the first of October and increase rapidly in frequency, peaking about the third week in October. They hold that level until about the second week of November, when they decrease rapidly, ending entirely or almost entirely about the first week of December.

Scrapes here appear suddenly about the third week of October, peak rapidly near the end of October, and sustain that approximate level until about November 15, dying out quickly after that.

The incidence of visiting and reworking I witnessed for both rubs and scrapes was exceedingly low: less than 3 percent of rubs showed signs of reuse in the same year. Scrape reworking was less than 5 percent and occurred only on the very largest scrapes and those immediately adjacent to runways, i.e., closer than two yards.

What does all this tell us? A lot! University of Georgia researchers (Marchinton, Miller, Kile, Litchfield, et al.) conducted longitudinal studies over several years in which they varied key parameters of the herd—buck:doe ratio, nutritional plane, age-class structure, and deer density. Rub densities were calculated by walking precise transects, counting all rubs within nine meters of the transects, and computing densities mathematically.

They found a range of 183–580 rubs per square kilometer, depending on the year and changes in the herd structure. They assumed that scrape densities would vary similarly. Note that this is a 300 percent variation! Remember I said earlier that some writers, mainly from the South, believed that hunting was much more difficult when acorn crops were abundant? These studies at the University of Georgia also revealed that the incidence of sign making increased significantly during years of high acorn abundance. Such is not the case in southern Michigan, where I saw no detectable differences. It seems clear to me that the increase the Georgia researchers detected came about because of widespread separation of the deer when a large mast crop was present, and, as I mentioned, we don't see that separation here since we have so few and localized mast-bearing trees.

I duplicated the Georgia study, to the best of my ability, for three years in my area and consistently came up with figures well below theirs: 127–165 rubs per square kilometer. Reusage of both rubs and scrapes was consistently lower, too. This is the effect of our horribly skewed buck to doe ratio and an age-class structure in which approximately 70 percent of all antlered bucks are yearlings! Sadly, our bucks do not need to advertise very much.

Unless you know these key parameters of the herd structure, articles about hunting over scrapes and rub lines may be of little meaning and no help to you.

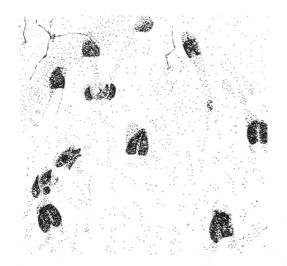

16

Deer Sign, Part II
Runways, Droppings, and
Tracks

I'm always surprised by how little scientific research has been done on the sign that deer create in their daily lives, other than rubs and scrapes. I suppose with research dollars as scarce as they are, I shouldn't be surprised, because in-depth research on sign may not shed all that much light on the whitetails' lives, as far as biologists are concerned. The subject of runways is a possible exception. Hunters, on the other hand, stand to benefit greatly from studying all visible clues about the whitetails' presence.

Everyone who writes about this kind of deer sign seems to have an opinion about it, but I don't recall a single reference that indicates scientific study. These opinions seem to be based on casual observation or on regurgitation of long-held beliefs, passed on from one person to another over the years. Are they valid? I seriously doubt it.

When I began my study, I resolved to conduct it for three years before writing up my findings. While I am pretty pleased with the majority of my study, when it comes to the matter of runways, droppings, and tracks, I know I've just scratched the surface, so to speak. By the time you are reading this book, I hope I will have found some more answers. In the meantime, here's what I've already learned.

Deer runs are every bit as "alive" and evolving as the animals that create them! One that's heavily used today may be abandoned tomorrow with a change in food source, weather, hunting pressure, precipitation or lack thereof, as well as untold other causes.

RUNWAYS

What we've read for years would lead us to expect that runways are static, basically unchanging entities. I decided to investigate this. I picked out twenty-five-yard sections of four different runs near my house and checked on them weekly. I did this for two consecutive years. I used these definitions: "no sign" meant no tracks, no droppings, and no disturbance of the duff; I used "little sign" when there were few tracks, no (or only very few) droppings, and minimal disturbance of the duff; "moderate sign" stood for tracks every foot or so, some droppings, and very noticeable disturbance of the soil and/or duff; I considered a run to show "heavy sign" when the tracks were almost continuous, had frequent droppings (every ten yards or less), and the disturbance of the soil and/or duff was continuous or very nearly so.

Runway #1

This run comes right up to the edge of a side road that has rather thick, brushy cover on the side with the run, and an open pasture a half-mile wide on the other.

The run showed little or no usage unless the deer were making a lot of long-distance movements. In other words, from mid-January, when there was snow pack of about five inches or more, there was hardly any usage at all. If the snow pack diminished or melted altogether, usage picked up slightly; if, in addition, the weather was moderate compared with what is normal for this area, usage was greater but still not heavy, only moderate at most.

Once snow pack diminished in the early spring, usage of this run went from little or none to heavy, literally overnight. This heavy usage continued for three or four weeks, diminishing somewhat as spring green-up began in earnest and falling to a low level once the does had separated themselves.

From about mid-May to mid-July, this run sometimes disappeared completely because of the tremendous growth rate of vegetation. When it reappeared in mid-summer, it re-formed in exactly the same place, running exactly the same course as the year before. It would be interesting to know how the deer determine where the run was before and why they re-form the run so precisely.

From mid-July to the first of September, usage of this run always varied from little to moderate, never heavy. Then, beginning when the bucks' antlers harden in mid-September, the level of usage jumped to heavy and remained heavy until the end of the year.

The heavy level of usage of this run was gratifying, but 90 percent of all activity on this runway at all times of year occurred at night. The slight daytime usage occurred, most frequently, during the mid to late winter and very early in the day in spring and autumn.

Runway # 2

This run leads through moderately thick brush, which funnels deer from a stand of thick planted pines, where the deer often bed and shelter, to either an open strip of hardwoods (maples, elms, no mast-bearing trees) or to an area of crop fields where the deer frequently feed.

This runway showed light to moderate usage all winter, falling to light or none if there was significant snow pack. Without snow pack, the usage level varied between light and heavy. In very early spring, usage was heavy, but in late spring, even though its surface was duff covered with little vegetative growth, for about six weeks one could lose sight of it entirely because there was no usage at all.

The rest of the year, from mid-July on, usage of this run was high, from moderate to heavy all the time.

Runway #3

This run travels along the crest of a ridge in a hardwood woodlot of mostly oaks, maples, and beeches. It was, early in my study, one of the most heavily used runways I found. Starting in early autumn, when my observations began, it remained heavily used that year until midwinter, when usage fell to between light and moderate. By spring, it showed no usage whatsoever and, with rare exception, it remained unused for the remainder of the two years of my study.

That first year was 1991, the year of the very heavy acorn crop I've described earlier, followed by a complete acorn failure the next two years. Following leaf drop the second year of my study, I could not see this run at all and would have missed it entirely if I had not marked it off the year before.

Runway #4

This run leads through thick brush that lies between two hardwood woodlots about a hundred yards apart. The deer often use this brush as a bedding area.

Until midwinter this run showed moderate to heavy use. From midwinter, usage decreased to little or none until very early spring, when it again showed very heavy usage. A few weeks later, however, at full green-up, the run showed little or no use and this level continued until around July first. For the rest of the year, usage levels vacillated between moderate and heavy.

I had an unexpected dividend in observing this run. During the second year of my study someone put up a tree stand only twenty yards from the run and placed a bait pile at about the same distance, but I could detect no difference in the amount of sign on the runway before and after the stand and bait appeared.

What do we learn from all of this? First and foremost, runways are anything but stagnant, unchanging entities. Their usage varies tremendously throughout the year and from one year to the next, evolving to reflect the lives of the animals that make, use, and maintain them.

During the late spring/early summer period, all runway use seems to decline greatly, with many, if not most, lying entirely unused. Just because deer live in close proximity to a runway does not mean they'll use it. Conversely, just because a runway isn't being used doesn't mean there are no deer living right there. Runways #1 and #3 had deer living in the surrounding area, but fell into disuse—Runway #3 so much so that it could not be seen at all.

Some runways seem to have a single purpose. For example, Runway #1 was used only when the deer were making long-distance movements of a half mile or a mile across an open pasture. During late winter and again in late spring/early summer, when they don't make that movement, the run is not used at all.

Runway #3 was used heavily when acorns were present for the deer to feed on, but without acorns, the run was completely abandoned, even though the deer were using the woodlot itself.

I recorded in detail the usage of these four runways, but during my study I followed literally hundreds of others. When I cut a runway, I chose one direction or the other and followed it until it ended or splintered or merged with other runways and I couldn't really say for sure that I was still on the same runway.

From this activity I learned some important lessons. In most cases I don't think it's meaningful to speak of a runway, but rather of runway systems. Very rarely does a single runway take you anywhere, but a system of runways can. In this respect, these runway systems are analogous to our own roadway systems.

I don't know if it's the same in all areas, but in southern Michigan only rarely can one follow a runway for long before it splinters or merges. Also, a section that is heavily used may change within the space of a hundred yards or less to a stretch of minimal usage.

Based on both numbers of runways and frequency of usage, it seems clear that in some areas runways are more important tools for the deer than elsewhere. Near water (ponds, swamps, and boggy areas) and in thick cover (tamarack and willow thickets or head-high fields of goldenrod) runways are especially well developed and heavily used, if they are being used at all. In such areas, the runways are more likely to be in complete systems that allow for quick movement between perimeter and interior. Other areas, such as open hardwoods, planted pines, and some grassy/herbaceous growth areas, never seem to have as many runways or as much usage as those in heavy cover.

A very high percentage of runways, maybe 90 percent, are found in thick cover. If you come to the edge of an opening, the run usually ends. Yet there are some well-used runways that lie in open fields or open woodlots with little or no undergrowth. Why? This is just one of the many unanswered questions I have about runways.

On many occasions, even in low-light situations, I've seen runways that were startlingly visible. While archery hunting a couple years ago, I hunted the same stand several times during the course of the season. It was situated at the north end of a thick swampy area, and in order to get to it, I had to walk through a fallow field of high goldenrod interspersed with willow thickets. There were several runways in this area, most running in a north-south direction. Deer moved both ways on these runs in the late evenings, and I never knew for sure from which direction they might come. Several evenings, while walking out, down one of the runs, I noticed that the run stretching out in front of me had almost a glow to it. I'm sure the glow resulted from the angle at which the evening light struck it. Yet, turning around and walking the other way, the run was very difficult to see!

We often read that the advantage of runways is their high degree of visibility. But (assuming the deer see what we see), what advantage could there be if only one direction is visible, and the deer are just as likely to be moving in the direction of poor visibility? That question makes me think of another.

If runways are used by deer for rapid escape, as, again, we often read, then why is it that they don't always use them to escape when they are frightened?

On the runway I've described above, I was sitting in my stand just moments before dark in late October when I heard the sounds of deer running out in front of me. Suddenly a doe broke into the open about twenty yards away, on the major run that traverses the area. She stopped just inside the opening and looked back over her shoulder. I heard two or three short grunts. The buck was thirty yards behind, and, just like the doe, he stopped when he hit the opening. Unfortunately, a bush between him and me prevented a clean shot. By then the doe had gone far enough to be downwind, and, scenting me, she blew and took off, leaving the runway and slashing through the brush. Without hesitation, the buck followed suit.

If that is typical behavior (and I believe it is), the theory that runways are for rapid escape seems contradicted. Perhaps there are times when runways aid in ease of movement or escape, but my observations often fail to support that. There is a lot more to it that we do not yet understand.

Based on close observation over many years, here are some things I do know for sure about runways.

Runways appear gradually and proliferate in number as long as snow pack is present. Sometimes within hours of the first snowfall, but always within a day or so, runways appear in whatever core areas the deer are using. The longer the snow stays, the more runways appear in the core areas and along their perimeter.

Most of the time, runways are visual, not olfactory, highways. It is very rare to see a deer moving down a runway scenting the run. Usually they move with their heads up, clearly seeing, not smelling, where they are going.

While it is true that most runways do lead into and out of feeding and bedding areas, if you don't know where these areas are, the runways alone will not tell you. The runways themselves do not change character enough within feeding and bedding areas to alert you to their function; you must learn this by observing the deer, or other sign.

It will do no good to hunt a runway without making certain that it is currently active. Changes in food supply, bedding sites, weather, and/or hunting pressure may cause a run to be abandoned, with a shift to others that had been inactive only a short time before.

DROPPINGS

For three years I walked through the woods and fields carrying plastic bags, calipers, magnifying glass, and a ruler as I probed, counted, measured, and collected droppings. I kept assorted piles that I'd collected, scattered about my yard, arranged by date. I collected only fresh droppings, in most cases ones I'd seen the deer defecate. I learned a surprising amount from this.

Biologists tell us that deer defecate thirteen to twenty times a day, the quantity varying throughout the year

Table 16.1
Average size of deer droppings by month (in millimeters)

	Length	Width
January	14	8.5
February	15	9
March	15	9
April	11.5	7
May	11	7
June	11	7
July	11	7
August	11	7
September	12	7
October	12	8
November	13	8.5
December	13	8

February and March are the only times I've ever found individual pellets connected by fibrous strands, which is indicative of the amount of fiber in the deer's diet at that time (and perhaps of some dehydration).

"Cow-flop" droppings occur during two periods of the year. They are much more common in spring (mid-April to early May) than autumn (October), but reflective of the rapid dietary changes common to both periods. Green in color in spring—the only time deer droppings are green—brown in October.

depending on what and how much the deer are consuming at the time. It takes food anywhere from ten to twenty hours to pass through their system.

Seasonal variations are the most significant. In winter, for example, deer in the North that are eating a large percentage of hard-to-digest browse take longer to digest it than the foods they eat in May or August. If the deer are eating a large percentage of roughage, they'll pass out a higher proportion of what they take in and do so more quickly because roughage has a higher content of indigestible fibers that just pass through. If they're eating early spring grasses and forbs or autumn acorns, fruits, and berries, then a much higher percentage will be assimilated, and they'll pass less. This makes for variation in pellet size, and in the total mass of droppings at any one time.

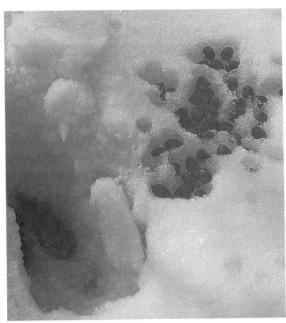

Deer droppings change in character throughout the year, by animal, by diet, by season, and by moisture content.

Winter

From late autumn into early winter (roughly mid-December to late January), the deer in my area eat pretty well. Individual droppings are relatively large, and the number of droppings per defecation is large, as well (see *Table 16.1*). As late winter sets in, the deer switch from grazing on crops, acorns, and forbs to a higher percentage of browse, and they eat less food overall. In addition, their metabolism slows down at this time. The results are that they defecate less often; but at the same time, because of increased fiber, the size of the individual pellets increases. These droppings are always very hard and well shaped.

During late winter I've observed something not seen at other times of year: the formation of continuous strands of pellets, that is, pellets connected together by long, fibrous strands. This is the result of the tremendously high fiber intake at this time, possibly aided by some degree of dehydration because water is locked up in the form of ice and snow and therefore less accessible to the deer.

The only time you'll see drop-pings of this nature (fibrous strands) are when the deer's diet is extremely high in fiber content and low in moisture.

Spring

We often speak of animals' ability or lack of ability to digest the various foods in their diet. Seldom do we take into account that animals do not digest their food alone. The alimentary tract (gut) is filled with microorganisms that do the actual digestion for insects, fish, birds, and mammals, including humans. Ruminants, such as deer, first shred the food fibers they eat and mix them with saliva, which helps to soften the fibers and to begin cleaving apart some of the proteins and complex carbohydrates. This combination of food and saliva further mixes with the microorganisms in the deer's gut. Each type of food requires different organisms to fully separate the complex chemical connections so that the deer can, at the end of the process, derive the best-possible nourishment from the foods consumed.

When deer have not eaten a particular class of food for a while, the specific organisms for that food decrease. If the deer begins to eat that food again, it takes some time for the organisms to build up so there are enough to do the job. The speed of this build-up depends on the type of food, the particular organism required, and the overall health of the deer. If the food change is sufficiently sudden or the deer sufficiently weakened, the microorganisms may not be able to build up in time, and the deer will perish. This is why we sometimes read of deer dying of starvation even though they have food stuffs in their paunches.

Artificial feeding programs can represent just such a sudden food change for the deer, and this is why the DNR does not feed deer artificially and recommends that no one else do so.

The reason for all this background is because in a typical year, deer experience no other food change as sudden and dramatic as the one that occurs every spring. Most dietary changes throughout the year are gradual; a food source diminishes as others emerge. But in spring, deer go overnight from a diet of twigs and buds (foods high in fiber but low in overall nutritive value) to a diet of fresh grasses and forbs (foods very low in fiber and bulk but extremely high in protein).

This change in diet produces a change in droppings that is more noticeable than at any other time of year.

Only twice a year are "cow flops" seen: frequently but not commonly, in autumn, if there's a major dietary change; and annually, in spring, after green-up. Cow-flop stools are routine for at least a couple of weeks each spring.

Throughout the rest of the year, deer droppings are usually in the form of the familiar football-shaped pellets, with anywhere from forty to two hundred pellets per movement. They are almost always in the range of brown to jet black. In very early spring, however, loose, nonformed "cow-flop" droppings are common, and, in fact, for the first couple of weeks of green-up, they constitute the majority of fresh droppings. When fresh, these cow-flop droppings are green and watery.

As the deer's microorganisms adjust, the more familiarly shaped pellets begin to replace the nonformed cow flops; however, the green color of the fresh droppings remains throughout the spring period. Lasting until perhaps early June, the green color is the surest way to know the dropping is fresh. Green-colored droppings invariably turn black within a matter of hours. If you find green droppings, you know they were passed within the previous twelve hours. Even after exposure to air turns the surface of the droppings to black, if you turn the droppings over and find a green underside, you know they are no more than a day or so old. No other time of year furnishes such a definitive indication of the age of a dropping.

Summer

Well-formed, moderate-size brown or black droppings are the rule all summer. By early summer the deer adopt basically the same diet they'll be on for the next two months, and digestion becomes easy as the microorganisms are totally adjusted and water is plentiful.

Autumn

In early autumn the deer undergo the second largest dietary change of the year. Since spring they've been eating crops, grasses, and other forbs; now, quite rapidly (over perhaps a one-month period), they begin consuming foods that are very high in carbohydrates—corn kernels, acorns, berries, and other fruits. Now, in October and early November, is when you'll begin to see brown cow flops. These brown droppings are not as numerous as the green cow flops of spring, but they constitute a high percentage of the autumn droppings. They begin to appear quite suddenly, then gradually diminish over the next month or five weeks. Other autumn droppings, brown or black, are of moderate size and normal shape.

I used to believe that the largest deer produced the largest droppings. I no longer believe this—or, at least, I know that other factors are much more important than size alone. These other factors that determine the size of droppings include: what the deer is eating (roughage/fiber increases the size); the percentage of moisture in their diet; how long the deer have been on a particular diet (the longer they're on it, the more adjusted to it they are, and so they'll assimilate it better and produce less waste); and any physiological stress the deer are under (pregnancy, lactation, antler growth, pelage change, illness or injury). All of these impact on digestion and, therefore, on stool production.

Remember the piles of droppings in my yard that I'd dated and monitored? I learned from that project that droppings last a lot longer than I'd have thought, and the speed of their disintegration is a complex issue. Overall it takes at least two months for droppings to disintegrate. Droppings that are in standing water or are intermittently (but consistently) wetted disintegrate fastest, and droppings that are lying on acidic soils (under conifers, for example) disintegrate faster than droppings on other soil types. Once they begin to disintegrate, they do so quickly, often in a matter of days.

If someone tries to tell you that they know how to determine the age of droppings, don't believe them. It's extremely difficult! The task is confounded by changes due to what the deer ate, moisture content, and how firm the droppings were when initially passed. Some experts claim to be able to age droppings by squeezing them; they'll often be wrong. A sheen or fresh appearance (a claim I've read) may be misleading. I've seen hundreds of droppings that appeared fresh after being moistened by dew, even though they were weeks old!

I've often read that droppings change from black to brown as they age, and this *may be true*, but they will also occasionally change from brown to black. Normally, droppings do not leach out their color over time and become paler; often a medium brown dropping will become much darker when moistened. I've never seen a deer dropping leach out the way dog droppings do. If deer droppings are continuously moist, especially in the autumn when the deer are eating berries and other fruits, they can become encased in mold, which makes them appear white—the only time I've ever seen white deer droppings.

All of this is bad news if you're a hunter, trying to age droppings. The good news is that there are a few things you can rely on. Fresh droppings *always* have a sheen and a smooth appearance; old droppings *may*. Any dropping without sheen or with ragged edges is old. Fresh droppings have a certain "spring" to them, or they will stay together, simply flattening when crushed. Old droppings tend to be desicated so they will not depress when squeezed; if old enough, they will just disintegrate when squeezed.

TRACKS

Practically any book or article about deer will tell you that big bucks have big feet and therefore make big tracks. Most articles go further and say that if you're really serious about getting a big buck, the most important first step is to find a big track. Is this true? Well, to be honest, yes and no.

Every year Michigan biologists check thousands of deer at state check stations. No other group I know has more experience in seeing truly big deer. Jim Hammill of Crystal Falls has been checking deer for twenty-two years, and his beliefs pretty well represent those of the biologists I've spoken to. He says, "Really big, mature bucks always have those big, wide, rounded-off feet. I've never seen an exception to that. However, you take a big six-, seven-, nine-year-old doe, and she'll have big feet, too. Whereas, even exceptional two- and even three-year-old bucks probably won't have those big feet. You wouldn't look at the feet of one of those deer and say, 'Wow, that's a big buck!'"

That's my experience, too, and it gets back to the issue of traditional deer management versus quality deer management I discussed earlier. The percentage of truly big, mature bucks in Michigan is very small—less than 1 percent. If you devote your time to looking for big tracks in a state like Michigan (or any other region with traditional deer management), you'll look for a long time without success. Your chances are better in areas like Michigan's western U.P., northern Wisconsin, parts of Minnesota, Maine, and remote mountainous regions of Vermont, New York, and Virginia, but even in those places your chances are slim.

In regions where deer have a very high nutritional plane (usually agricultural areas), one finds that the vast majority of "really big bucks" taken are two- and three-year-old animals that have extremely nice racks and big bodies—some over two hundred pounds—with only modest foot size.

In November 1993 a world record "typical" buck was taken by Milo Hanson, a farmer from Saskatchewan, Canada. In *Outdoor Life* (April 1994) Jim Zumbo reports Mr. Hanson's frustration while hunting this animal because despite his immense size, his party couldn't track the buck since his foot size was nothing out of the ordinary. Every time the buck went into an area with other deer, they'd lose him because there was nothing distinctive about his track. This despite the fact that the buck shattered an eighty-year world record by more than seven inches of total mass. The buck turned out to be only three and a half years old—in other words, an immature buck despite his great size.

The key in all this is the word "mature." Mature deer, that is, deer four years of age or more, normally have big feet whether they are does or bucks. Their hooves are worn, rounded, and wide—some are over three inches wide—but they're extremely rare. So rare that it's a waste of good hunting time to search for them.

During my study, I carefully measured hundreds of tracks (see *Table 16.2*) Not one in three years' time even came close to the three-inch width we read about. Maybe those writers that talk about hunting big tracks don't think our eight-, ten-, twelve-, or even fourteen-point southern Michigan deer are worth hunting, but I know that every year I see some incredible Michigan bucks—with dainty little feet. Here, if you want to hunt impressive deer, you can forget about hunting for impressive tracks.

Table 16.2
Average track size in inches

Length	Width	Range
3¼	2⅛	2⅜ to 3½ long
		1¼ to 2⅜ wide

I only measured tracks of deer walking, with toes together, in soft soil or snow less than one inch deep. I only measured tracks between August and May each year to negate the influence of newborn fawns on average track size.

17

Weather and Whitetails

In the 1994 edition of my book *The Deer Hunter's Field Guide: Pursuing Michigan's Whitetail*, I devoted a chapter to the effects of weather on various hunting techniques and strategies. After three years of intense study of deer reaction to weather, I am able to confirm everything I said, and I can now add some additional items.

The effects of weather on deer behavior are very, very difficult to understand and predict. This is because weather seems to have a different impact depending on the time of year and, therefore, what the deer's agenda is; that is, the biological tasks and necessities they have to accomplish. How deer react to a set of weather conditions is not necessarily how they'll react the next time those weather conditions appear similarly, even if the next time is the very next day! We can describe tendencies and predict probabilities, but we cannot accurately predict overall behavior.

In my three-year field work, I studied several parameters of weather daily, including wind velocity and direction, precipitation, temperature, barometric pressure, humidity, and cloud cover. I added phases of the moon, as well.

I kept a running table of those factors, and the date, total number of deer seen, number of tracks counted on my daily surveillance of a mile-long, dead-end country road, and number of deer Annette and I counted on our drive each evening.

WIND

The general assumption is that wind, more than any other weather feature, dictates deer behavior on any given day. This is partly true, but whoever is in charge of the department of general assumptions forgot to tell the group of eleven deer I watched on February 15, 1991.

My notes from that observation say, "The weather has been horrible for the past forty-two hours. It started to snow at 9:00 P.M. on 2-13-91, and it hasn't stopped yet. We now have roughly seven inches of snow on the ground. Last evening at about 7:00, the wind began to blow and the temperature began to drop. It got down to twelve degrees last night with 25 mph winds and blowing snows. Now it's eleven degrees with 24 mph winds, gusting to 32 mph out of the northwest. Windchill is minus thirty-five degrees!

"Out from 10:00 A.M. until 2:30 P.M. I saw no signs in the big pasture, but I saw sign practically everywhere else. I saw deer and deer tracks, even in the open, but always near cover and always in areas protected from the wind. I also saw tracks within the cover.

"I watched eleven deer for forty-one minutes. They didn't know I was there. Much of the time they fed; particularly the younger, smaller animals seemed to feed without concern. Also, they showed a lot of grooming behavior—perhaps 10 percent of the time—both individual and mutual.

"I saw two episodes of aggression, high-head stare and low-head rush, both directed at a younger deer that had been acting rather frisky.

"While I watched, four of the deer lay down. None attempted to scrape out a bed; they just lay down, close to one another (three to ten feet apart). They didn't face each other; each faced essentially the same direction: downwind."

Later the same day, for thirty-three minutes I watched two deer feed "... in the oaks right near ——'s deer stand. They fed the entire time, never moving outside an area about eighteen by twenty-five feet. There were no signs of aggression. At least one of them was a buck; I could see his pedicles (he had no antlers). After I ran them off, I back-tracked and found three other places where they'd rooted for acorns and grass. All four areas measured about twenty by twenty-five feet. In between the deer showed no attempt to find food, though the areas where they fed looked no different to me from the areas they walked right past."

I include these entries in their entirety because they illustrate how, despite high winds, the deer were active. The second illustrates my point made earlier about deer being most active in the middle of the day in winter (or the warmest portion of the day). The entries also illustrate the selective feeding patterns of deer, sometime feeding for long periods of time in confined areas, yet by-passing other, seemingly identical food plots. The entries also illustrate quite nicely the kinds of behaviors I looked for and recorded in the notes of my daily observations.

After reviewing the notes of my observations, I concluded that the effect of wind on deer actually depends on several variables. The most important of these is the time of year. Wind has a more pronounced effect on deer behaviors in late autumn and winter than at any other time of year. I believe this is because during the hunting seasons the deer feel threatened, and if the deer are being pressured, then wind is much more likely to curtail their activities.

Remember the window of opportunity with regard to breeding and the birth of fawns? That isn't the only window period for deer. There are certain tasks the deer must accomplish at different times of the year, if they are to flourish. The difficulty of these tasks varies, according to the dictates of each habitat. For example, a process called lipogenesis (accumulation of body fat) is essential in the autumn if the deer in the North are to survive the rigors of winter. The procurement and assimilation of nutrients in the spring so the doe can successfully complete her pregnancy is another. When a deer is faced with an absolute necessity like one of these, I'm convinced the deer finds a way to do it, no matter how windy it is. Deer activity may slow down or even come to a halt for a time, but high winds do not keep a deer down for long.

TEMPERATURE

Except for the autumn to winter transition when the deer become acclimated to colder conditions or, to some degree, in the harshest part of winter itself or a particularly cold snap in the spring, I don't find that temperature has much impact on deer behavior in southern Michigan. At other times, we seldom experience severe temperatures in either direction, and the deer's nutritional plane is so high and the availability of water so abundant, that temperature simply does not disrupt their daily routine.

Other regions may witness more temperature-related behavioral change. Extreme heat, especially in combination with high humidity, is likely to alter deer behavior throughout the South. Extremely bitter temperatures in the far North, especially in an area with low-quality food base, will, of course, have a dramatic impact on deer behaviors.

Light to moderate precipitation, especially in conjunction with mild or moderate temperatures and the invariably lower light levels, will often invoke heightened activity and movement.

PRECIPITATION

Light precipitation rarely has any appreciable effect. Unless combined with high wind or extreme cold, even heavy precipitation may not dampen deer activity levels. In fact, heavy snows in late autumn or early winter often heighten activity. The longer precipitation is sustained, the less effect it has. If it lasts over ten or fifteen hours, the deer get on with their activities, unaffected. If such a precipitation is combined with high wind or extreme cold, the deer will take to cover, but they'll carry on their activities nonetheless.

BAROMETRIC PRESSURE

Changes in barometric pressure normally precede pronounced weather changes. The general belief is that animals somehow sense weather changes before they occur, perhaps because of the barometric pressure. This issue highlights the difficulty in teasing out the variables in the effects of weather on deer behaviors. Seldom can one isolate barometric pressure changes independent of weather changes, and on those rare occasions when this is possible, the results are not what you'd expect. Look at *Table 17.1* and notice several days on which barometric pressure dropped 0.20 millimeters or more. Note that two of these decreases are accompanied by attendant decreases in deer sightings and apparent activity levels, but one of them (on the thirteenth) is just the opposite. Similarly, barometric pressure increases of 0.20 millimeters or more are usually accompanied by increases in deer activity and sightings, but not always (see February 15).

HUMIDITY

In his 1992 book *Hunting Trophy Whitetails*, Dick Morris speculates that in the sometimes oppressive heat of the South high humidity depresses deer activity. I certainly agree with that, but I see no evidence that humidity is a significant determinant of deer behavior in most areas, outside the South. As with barometric pressure, it is exceedingly difficult to separate the effects of humidity from those of other

Table 17.1 Weather features versus total number of deer seen

Date	Number of Deer		Precipitation/ Major Weather	Temperature Range	Wind Velocity	Barometric Pressure
	on Walk	on Drive				
February 1	0		no/sunny	10 to 45	extremely high	30.34
2	0	6	no/sunny	7 to 26	moderate	30.19
3	0	18	no/sunny	16 to 42	mod. to very hi	30.50
4	0	26	no/sunny	18 to 40	light to mod.	30.10
5	0	2	no/sun/ovct*	24 to 40	mod. to high	30.21
10	2	14	snow/overcast			30.34
11	0	8	snow			30.09
12	0	2	snow/overcast			29.71
13	0	7	snow/overcast	5 to 20	light to mod.	29.93
14	0	10	no/overcast	17 to 31	mod. to very hi	29.98
15	4	25	snow/overcast	10 to 26	extremely high	30.24
16	0	0	snow/overcast	10 to 29	mod. to extr. hi	29.91
17	0	0	snow/overcast	0 to 28	mod. to extr. hi	30.21
18	6	6	no/partly sun	-5 to 10	light to mod.	30.09
19	0	1	no/sunny	-7 to 20	calm to mod.	30.10
20	0	2	no	7 to 25	extremely high	29.99
21	3	3	snow/overcast	0 to 20	light to mod.	29.63
22	0	4	snow/overcast	3 to 25	light to mod.	29.51
23	2	12	snow/overcast	14 to 15	light to mod.	29.91
24	3	6	no/sunny	-2 to 15	hi to very hi	30.21
26	2	8	no/sunny	0 to 22	light to mod.	30.33
27	0	0	no/sunny	-5 to 26	light to mod.	30.38
28	0	0	no/ sunny	-3 to 30	light to high	30.31

*no precipitation sunny to overcast

The data I accumulated regarding weather over a three-year period is illustrated in this one-month example. It indicates, more than anything else, just how difficult it is to study, and attempt to predict, weather-related factors upon deer behavior. In regions with generally benign weather patterns, such as southern Michigan, the deer's overall task needs at any given time will much more profoundly affect their behaviors than will weather, barometric pressure, and/or phases of the moon. Furthermore, the more persistent any given weather feature, the more the deer tend to ignore it and get on with their normal activities.

weather-related factors. In three years of tracking deer and recording weather in southern Michigan, I found not a single incident of humidity having an impact on deer behaviors.

CLOUD COVER

When it diminishes the effects of a harsh sun, cloud cover could heighten deer activity levels. Conversely, if it serves to trap heat and humidity, cloud cover could serve to depress activity when it's hot or heighten it when it's cold. That sounds reasonable, but, in fact, I've not found much correlation, and I have no reason to believe there is one in such a benign region as ours in southern Michigan.

MOON PHASES

The data in *Table 17.2* indicates the typical annual cycle of deer behaviors under the conditions in southern Michigan. I included the number of sightings per day charted against the phases of the moon. The figures do not support an interpretation that the moon influences behavior, and this is my gut feeling, too. Sixty percent of the time in the Great Lakes region, cloud cover is so heavy as to block the moonlight altogether or enough to negate its effect. Many writers and some researchers have speculated that the moon's influence is more potent in the South during autumn because of their longer breeding seasons. The belief is that when there's heightened pressure on the deer and they have the luxury of time, they utilize moonlight to carry on mating. That may be romantic, but I don't believe it's true; the imperative is to breed the does when they cycle in, and there's no reason to think the cycle is in any way related to lunar phases. The doe's twenty-eight-day cycle is not in sync with any phase of the moon.

Throughout much of October, November, and early December much deer activity is shifted to nighttime hours, whether full moon or otherwise, under the pressures brought on by hunting and poaching, as I've discussed earlier. In January, February, and until the weather breaks in March, their metabolic rates (and hence overall activity level) are lowered. At that time, their entire mode of functioning is geared toward conserving their energies. From some time in

April through September we see heightened, almost exaggerated, activity levels as the deer take advantage of the abundance of food available. I believe this annual cycle is carried out by the deer with very little modification due to weather or lunar change.

If you are attempting to hunt, observe, or photograph deer, you'll need to take into account the various parameters of the weather, but it seems clear to me that much of what's written (and therefore believed) conforms to the comfort and perspective of humans, not to the legitimate facts of deer life.

Table 17.2 Moon phase influence on number of deer seen

	Date	Number of Deer Seen	Moon Phase
September	1	17	full moon
	2	0	
	3	36	
	4	38	
	5	29	
	6	36	
	7	13	
	8	30	last quarter
	9	1	
	10	19	
	11	52	
	12	46	
	13	18	
	14	42	
	15	43	new moon
	16	1	
	17	28	
	18	27	
	19	34	
	20	33	
	21	42	
	22	31	first quarter
	23	41	
	24	55	
	25	66	
	26	30	
	27	0	
	28	9	
	29	4	
	30	7	full moon

In an attempt to better understand any possible influence of the phases of the moon on deer behavior and/or activity, I took the specific day each month when that particular phase was at its zenith, and then considered the previous three days and the following three days. Therefore, each phase of the moon, each month, has a range of seven consecutive days. To be clear, look at September 15, 1993. This was the night of the new moon—the dark phase of the moon. Adding the three days prior and the three days following, we have the new moon phase spanning September 12 to September 18, inclusive. The total number of deer seen each month, during each phase, was then added and divided by the total number of days of observation to yield an "average number of deer seen per day." By conducting this study for three consecutive years, I saw wild fluctuations in these monthly averages. Some months more deer were seen under the influence of the full moon, some under the influence of the new moon, or either the last or first quarter moon. There was no discernible consistency to this pattern; neither by month, nor by season, nor annually.

My conclusion is that no correlation exists between moon phase and the number of deer seen per day. There is an important reason for adding the caveat, "at lease in southern Michigan." On an annual basis, cloud cover in the Great Lakes region runs greater than 60 percent. During the months of November, December and January, this percentage jumps to more than 90 percent. During May, June, July and August it is near 20 percent. The cloud cover, at least in this region, is therefore a complication not easily overcome or understood. My belief is that, if there is a moon-phase effect on deer behavior in this area, the study designed to demonstrate it would need to run far longer than three years. My gut feeling, however, is that even if there is a moon-phase effect on deer behavior/activity levels, the effect is much less than that of many other factors.

There is yet another, even more compelling, reason why I have serious doubts about moon-phase-related effects on deer activity levels. In the 1994 edition of *A Practical Guide to Producing and Harvesting White-Tailed Deer*, author James Kroll states that some researchers believe that whitetail see in dim light one hundred thousand to one million times better than man. While not all researchers may believe the whitetail to have night vision that acute, all agree that the deer's capabilities are manyfold better than man's. I can't help but wonder, if deer do indeed have those levels of capability, why would moonlight make any difference to them at all? I honestly doubt it does.

Bedding Behaviors

One of my neighbors farms a thirty-acre field near my house. Often he has this field planted in a clover mixture. One section of the field is well secluded because of the roll of the land. There is plenty of escape cover, isolation from the highway, and protection from the wind. The deer love it! Every year when my neighbor goes to hay, his story is the same, "The deer have just torn the —— out of that area! They eat that stuff like it's candy. I counted thirty-five beds just in that little section over the hill." Then he laughs. Typical of most of the farmers I've known, he resents that the deer try to eat him out of house and home and that they lay all over his field, mashing it down so his thrasher can't harvest it, but he loves the deer and clearly enjoys having them around.

I don't know if my neighbor knows it, but the only time the deer are in his field continuously is when it's growing just before harvest. Studies have shown that some amount of disturbance and pruning actually stimulates some plants to grow faster—just like cutting your grass in the spring makes it grow that much faster—but what crop fields cannot bounce back from so quickly is being trampled and flattened. So, often it's not feeding, but bedding by deer that causes the damage, at least in some types of crop fields.

I tried to keep track of where and when the deer bedded during my three-year study, and I counted a total of more than seventeen thousand beds.

WINTER

Wind is the key to where deer bed in winter. They try to minimize their heat loss by avoiding the brunt of the wind. Research has shown a difference (more marked, of course, in autumn and winter) between daytime and nighttime bedding sites (Marchinton and Jeter 1967). Daytime beds are generally in thicker cover and most frequently in the deer's core area. Nighttime beds are more often in or immediately adjacent to feeding areas; however, I found that in winter the nighttime beds were almost always in cover, too. Less than 2 percent of the winter beds I found were in the open.

For three years I kept records of all the beds I located, noting the date, whether they were on hillsides or flatlands, in cornfields, hayfields, fallow fields, swamps, open woodlots, planted pines, or brush. I also noted whether they were

Table 18.1 Bedding Sites
Bedding sites by location through the year with one being most preferred and seven being least preferred

	Planted Pines	Brush	Open Hardwood	Mixed Woodlots	Near Edge
Winter	1	2	4	3	85%
Spring	6	4	5	3	50%
Summer	7	6	4	5	50%
Fall	4	2	5	3	100%

	Crop Fields	Fallow Fields	Ravines Adjacent area	Hills
Winter	7	6	5	85%
Spring	2	1	7	30%
Summer	3	2	1	30%
Fall	7	6	1	40%

Bedding Sites

During the winter period (by which I mean there's snow pack of five inches or more, from late December through mid- to late March), bedding preferences were very marked, with planted pines, brushy areas, mixed woodlots, and either dry marshes or high ground areas in wetter marshes exhibiting more than 90 percent of all bedding activity, day or night. Open woodlots showed roughly 7 percent of bedding, while fallow fields and crop fields showed less than 2 percent. Over 85 percent of all winter bedding sites will be found in the immediate vicinity of hillsides too. I found little consistency in just where on the hillsides the deer would bed, but the beds would clearly be associated with them.

During spring, fallow fields and crop fields witnessed a very rapid and tremendous increase in usage, becoming the favored bedding sites, while planted pines, marshy areas, and brush witnessed the largest decreases. These changes represent the second most dramatic bedding site changes of the entire year; they'll occur in a matter of days when snow pack levels diminish, and spring green-up begins. Hillsides become far less important. I couldn't detect a noticeable difference in daytime/nighttime sites, except that daytime areas were more likely to be in areas shielded from human intrusion/activity.

In summer, riverine plains, marshes and ponds (within two hundred feet) become the preferred bedding sites. Shade is sought. Fallow fields are heavily used as are crop fields, especially at night. Hillside usage is variable, more common on warmer and windier days.

In autumn, bedding site changes are very dramatic and sudden, more so than any other time of the entire year (at least in southern Michigan), as poaching pressures mount in early September. Open areas, especially during the day, are abandoned. Heavy cover is the key to survival, especially for bucks. It's not just the edges of cover, however, that are utilized, as at other periods when heavy cover is sought; instead, the interiors of heavy cover are utilized, much more so than at any other time of the year. Almost all bedding is within thirty feet of an edge. It cannot be overemphasized: escape cover is critical now.

in the interior portions of cover or within thirty feet of an edge. My findings are presented in *Table 18.1*.

You will notice that more than 85 percent of all beds found in January, February, and most of March were located within thirty feet of an edge. Generally that meant an interface between brush and a crop field, for example, but it could also mean an area of heavier brush or other ground cover within an open woodlot. Whenever and wherever the habitat changes, that's where the deer will most generally bed.

Another clear finding is that more than 85 percent of the time, the deer will bed on a hillside. I found no reliable

Favored bedding sites vary be season, as well as by level of interference and disruption, in relation to cover. They vary in relation to their proximity to hillsides too, depending upon season, time of day, and weather. They vary by the deer's sex, age, and experience; older bucks invariably bed closer to, if not in, cover year-round, especially daytime beds.

indication of where on the hillside they'll choose to bed. It seems to depend on several variables, including wind, snow depth, grade of the hill, exposure to the sun, if any, and perhaps other factors not apparent to me. I found that deer utilize different parts of hillsides for bedding, most often choosing the top or bottom third and avoiding the middle sections unless there's a bench (flat spot) on them.

In winter I found that they bed about an equal number of times in open hardwoods, mixed woods, brush, and planted pines; however, that is misleading since in my area only about 5 percent of the woods are in the form of planted pines, and woodlots are four times more numerous than brushy areas. Therefore, the true order of bedding preference is planted pines, brush, and then woodlots (with mixed woodlots twice as likely to be used as hardwoods). Next came swamps, but this was not consistent since some swamps were totally abandoned by the deer while others were continuously used. The deciding factor seemed to be whether the swamp had fluctuating water levels; those that did were vacated. As I mentioned, crop fields were rarely utilized for winter bedding—less than 2 percent of the time.

I've often read that deer paw away the snow from a bedding site. In fact I've read it so often, I supposed that it's usually the case. However, in examining over five thousand winter bedding sites and personally watching more than two hundred deer bed down with snow cover present, I witnessed only two deer paw out their beds and saw evidence of such pawing behavior in less than 1 percent of the beds I examined. So, while I have to confirm that it does happen, I'd have to conclude that it's the exception, not the rule. Perhaps it's habitual for certain individual deer, which would certainly be an interesting phenomenon.

Shelter from the wind, and hence wind chills, is critical in winter.

SPRING

Changes in springtime bedding behavior do not necessarily coincide with our concept of spring but rather with the disappearance of snow pack and the very beginnings of green-up.

Winter bedding patterns are the most easily known and studied because the deer are so confined in winter (90 percent of the deer may be living on 10 percent of the land mass), they're living in bigger groupings than at any other time of year, and that is when snow pack is most frequently present. At other times, it is much harder to collect data on bedding because it's easier to miss beds when there's no snow. Still, because of the time and effort I devoted to my study, I'm very confident in the accuracy of my findings.

In very early spring, fallow fields and brushy areas within 150–200 feet of ponds and swamps see the earliest increases in bedding activity. The deer seek these areas for both daytime and nighttime bedding. Simultaneously, bedding in the planted pines and brushy areas preferred in winter decreases dramatically. As green-up spreads to other areas, bedding sites spread out, too. Hillsides aren't nearly as preferred as in winter; deer are likely to bed almost anywhere in late spring and early summer. Open areas are utilized a lot, but the lion's share of beds is still to be found near the edges, where two or more types of habitat abut.

SUMMER

Early summer is the most difficult time to determine precise bedding sites. The vegetation is so thick and the deer so spread out in small groups that it appears they bed just about anywhere and everywhere. With some relatively minor exceptions, that is true. They will bed near water more frequently than elsewhere, and in areas where they can get respite from hordes of biting insects. Often this means finding shady areas and/or areas where they can be exposed to the wind—just the opposite of their winter pattern, when they attempt to avoid the wind and catch the sun.

By late summer, it's a little easier to find beds, as the far-flung, smaller groups begin to coalesce. Sites in the shade, near water, protected from tormenting bugs continue to be chosen.

AUTUMN

Near the end of September an abrupt and dramatic change occurs in my area. While nighttime beds continue to be in the open feeding areas, daytime beds suddenly shift to cover. Swamps, brush, and edges immediately adjacent to thick escape cover are the preferred daytime bedding sites.

This tendency becomes more and more exaggerated as hunting and poaching pressures mount until, by late October, almost all daytime bedding and a majority of nighttime bedding takes place within heavy cover. Edges are still important, but the interiors of cover are even more important, especially for older bucks. These patterns continue at least until early December, when the edges are once again preferred. After hunting/poaching pressure begins to abate, deer leave the swamps unless they have high ground. They begin to avoid the wind and look for sunlit areas within cover.

It cannot be overemphasized that bucks, especially mature bucks, do not bed in the open. This buck was in the company of a doe and her two fawns when I photographed him. The doe and fawns bedded in the open, he in the nearby brush!

The whitetail adheres to some habitual bedding behaviors. If not unduly harassed, an individual buck or a group of bucks tends to use the same small area of an acre or so for bedding. Wherever such a bedding area is located, the buck(s) will use it regularly, year in and year out (such areas are called "core areas" or "sanctuaries" and are much more important to bucks than does), although several such core areas will be used as the seasons progress (see *Diagram 18.2*). These areas always seem to have at least three characteristics that distinguish them from surrounding areas: (1) they're invariably in thick cover, (2) they have a nearby water supply, and (3) they have adjacent escape cover. Several researchers have noted that individual deer often use precisely the same bed site repeatedly.

Doe groups almost always tend to bed nearer their feeding sites than do bucks, hence does do not have core areas in the same sense bucks do. Does, therefore, use many more bedding areas than do bucks, especially daytime bedding areas.

When bedding, deer have their own individual routines they go through. Some, perhaps most, simply walk to the site, examine it briefly by sight and smell, and lie down. Others scrutinize the site more carefully, perhaps circling it once or twice and pawing a stick or something out of it. Sometimes a deer will just lie down on top of whatever happens to be there. I once found a bed with a large, jagged rock frozen in the ground. I'm talking about a six-inch rock, sticking up three or four inches out of the ground. The deer had simply lain on it, apparently for a long time.

Deer do not face each other when bedding in a group. They may face the same or opposite directions, but they avoid direct eye contact. Whether alone or in a group, deer most often face downwind. In this way, they can hear and smell whatever is behind them and see what is in front of them.

Deer usually bed with their heads up and their eyes open. I've seen only a half-dozen deer over the years with their heads lowered and maybe fifty with their eyes closed—but only for seconds at a time. Sometimes I've seen deer chewing on their cud, very relaxed, and it seemed they could barely keep their eyes open; they'd slowly close their

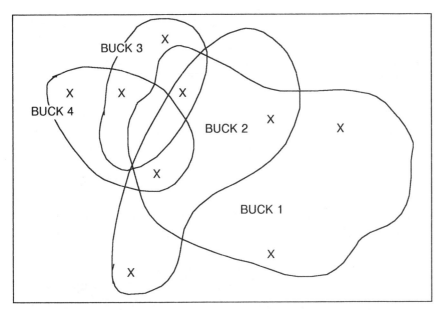

Lined areas represent home ranges. Xs represent sanctuaries

Diagram 18.2 Home Range Areas and Sanctuaries

This diagram is a schematic representation of the several overlapping home ranges and core areas (sanctuaries) of associated bucks. That labeled Buck 1 represents the most dominant or Alpha buck in the area. Generally, but not always, his home range will be larger than that of lesser bucks in the area.

Throughout much of the year these bucks will have frequent contact and, at times, high levels of interactions. They will be the various members of a "bachelor group." Each buck, within his home range (the larger, elliptical shaped areas), will have one or more sanctuaries or core areas from which he'll essentially center his activities. These areas may well change throughout the course of the year as food or water sources wax and wane, or as various doe groups, within the buck's range, cycle in or out of estrus. The size of home ranges can vary greatly. They may be only a couple hundred acres, or they may be several thousand. They will greatly expand during the various phases of the rut, and be larger than at any other time of the year. Several variables influence the size of the individual's range, including: dominance of the specific buck in question, deer densities, age structure of the herd, habitat quality, availability of water, and individual variation in the temperment of the specific buck. Bucks' home ranges are always larger than that of does, and within each buck's range there will be several doe groups.

Sanctuaries are those much smaller areas within the buck's range where he seeks shelter and safety. These areas offer him his greatest security, and he seeks them out when he feels threatened or needs solitude. While he may not utilize them every day, he will do so whenever he feels the need.

eyes for fifteen or twenty seconds, then reopen them. At such times, the deer would go on chewing, maybe turning their heads to look around, maybe not, then slowly closing their eyes again, to repeat the cycle. Once I watched a yearling in a group with four other deer, with its head down, curled up like a dog for about five minutes before it raised its head. I once shot a buck that was alone during the rut; he had been in this same posture, but I believe this is highly unusual.

When preparing to bed, a deer lowers itself one leg at a time to its front knees, then lowers its hind quarters by folding up the back legs in unison. To rise, it raises up on its front knees first, then raises its hind quarters, then rises on one front leg at a time. If the deer is startled, this action is so quick it looks like a single motion.

Frequently used bedding areas are invariably heavily soiled with droppings, as all deer habitually relieve themselves immediately upon rising, very often directly onto the bedding site. Deer will bed on soiled ground, especially in the "preferred" bedding sites I mentioned above. Even with a deer density in my study area as low as only fifteen to twenty deer per square mile, I've counted as many as 250 pellet piles in a "preferred" bedding area only about twenty feet by twenty feet! With such pellet densities, the deer couldn't really avoid bedding on soiled ground, and they do so with seeming unconcern. This, because of the bedding tendencies already discussed, is far more common in winter than any other time of the year.

19

The Use of Scents, Calls, and Rattling Techniques

Back in the early 1960s a friend of mine who has since passed away, Ed Borders, was invited to hunt a private club near Onaway. As I remember it, the club had 460 acres and took a half dozen hunters for the first week of gun season and another group the second week. The owner of the club had some very specific, rather strict rules. One was, when he put you on a stand, you stayed there until he came to get you. Period. Long before daylight on opening day, he took Ed to the end of a logging road and told him to walk straight ahead for a hundred yards or so and take a stand. This put Ed on the very end of the club property. Both behind him and to his right, there was state land, all very heavily hunted, and the deer could be expected to move back and forth on any of several runways in the immediate area.

Ed's excitement was short-lived. As the sky began to lighten, he heard disturbing noises—talking and laughter, banging and clanging—headed his way. As the noise drew nearer, Ed got quite annoyed. He could hardly believe his eyes as he saw four teenagers, two couples carrying a cooler, blankets, rifles, and God knows what else down the fenceline, farther into the woods. Since the kids were on state land and his host had told him not to move under any circumstances, he could do nothing but wait and watch.

The kids stopped at the corner of the fenceline a hundred yards away and decided to "hunt." For two hours, as Ed smoldered, the kids laughed and joked, playing loud rock 'n' roll music around a bonfire, the smoke from which drifted to Ed whenever the wind was right. Long after giving up any hope of seeing deer, Ed was startled when he heard shots fired by the kids. Over the general ruckus he heard the kids yelling, "You got him! Shoot again!" Ed heard running and laughter, and when one of the boys said something about how big he was, Ed couldn't stand it any longer. Rules or not, he had to go see what was going on.

The two boys were bent over a downed buck (I don't remember how big), dressing it out. The kids explained that they'd just looked up, and the buck was standing there looking at them.

In 1987 or 1988 my late friend Joe Frankum, one of the men this book is dedicated to, was hunting the Upper somewhere near the community of Ralph. He was hunting with two or three other guys, and it was decided they'd meet back at the van around noon for lunch. They'd parked early that morning off the side of a logging trail quite a way back in the woods. Joe got to the van before the others so he started to work on lunch. He set up a table and some folding chairs, started the coffee on a Coleman, and got out some lunch items. He heard a noise behind him, but thought little of it, figuring it was one of his buddies returning. He poured a cup of coffee and strolled over to where he'd propped his rifle. Glancing over toward the noise some forty yards away, Joe looked right at a buck, staring him in the face. Slowly reaching over and loading his gun, Joe shot the curious six-point!

I have related these two stories not because they contain any tidbits of deer hunting wisdom or insight, but precisely because they do not. No one could possibly think that lighting bonfires and playing rock 'n' roll music or moving about with careless, noisy nonchalance would lead to successful hunting. Yet every day hunters do things that are either neutral or even downright disruptive and are successful despite their antics. Oftentimes they even think their success was *because* of their behavior. Examples of these include horn rattling (in almost any region of the country with traditional deer management practices), putting out scents and lures (in regions with these practices), and calling.

Don't misunderstand, I'm not saying rattles, scents, lures, and calling never work. All I'm saying is they won't work unless you have the right circumstances, and those circumstances do not exist in a very large proportion of the whitetails' range. Whether we agree with their decisions or not, most game departments around the country have determined to manage their whitetail herds to equal or exceed the carrying capacity of their range, to overshoot the buck segment of their herds, to maximize deer kill figures, to maximize the number of "hunter-days" afield, and to maximize their income via license sales (see Chapter 9).

When you have a situation like the one in Michigan, where there's an almost total lack of competition among bucks for breeding rights, these hunting techniques of rattling, calling, and luring are extremely ineffective. These techniques rely on natural pressures (automatically present in a well-balanced deer herd) to ensure competition among bucks. Traditional management eliminates those pressures; there are so many does for every available buck that the bucks are not likely to respond to these various forms of "advertising."

Writing in the January 1994 issue of *Deer & Deer Hunting Magazine*, Charles Alsheimer says, "In theory, an adult buck should be able to breed four to seven adult females (Jackson 1973)." With adult does so far outnumbering bucks, there is no pressure and hence no response.

I don't claim to be a good rattler, but because of my experience over the years hunting in Georgia, South Carolina, Alabama, and Texas, I've successfully rattled in and killed five bucks. As part of my study of the past three years, I've attempted rattling on more than a hundred occasions in places the various "experts" say it should work. On four of these occasions, the deer were in sight and I witnessed their actual responses. Furthermore, I limited my rattling attempts to that period when it should be most effective, roughly October 15 to November 25 in southern Michigan. I did not rattle in a single deer, and in the four cases I could observe the deer's reactions, based on the way they ran, it looked for all the world like I had startled the devil out of them!

During the three-year study, I conducted more than three hundred controlled observations of deer response using various deer lures and other products, ranging from motor oil to household cleaning agents to human urine, always including, as a test control, a site with nothing added to it. These observations were controlled as follows.

A test site consisted of a patch of ground approximately five feet by five feet that was raked clear of all litter and duff so the ground was both exposed and softened. The substance to be tested was applied directly to the soil. On control sites, I did nothing beyond raking the site clear to expose the soil. Each series of tests contained five test sites, and I conducted each series for five consecutive days. I checked the site daily, recording the results, and refreshened the sites by raking them again and adding more of the substance being studied. Each site had a different substance, and that substance only would be used on that site all five days of the study.

For each test site I recorded the date, a description of the surrounding area, the presence or absence of nearby runways and how far they were from the site, and daily weather features. Each site was checked daily for signs of deer tracks. I made no further attempt to categorize the responses. Some sites had only one or a few tracks, others had many. Here are the results:

	Positive (percent)	Responses Positive (tracks present)	Negative (tracks not present)
Neutral test sites (nothing on them)	42	19	26
Commercial lures (includes deer urines)	35	56	104

Animal urines (other than deer)	43	15	20
Household items	20	7	28

I am fascinated by these results. It is an industry known for its wild claims—"Danger: Do not apply to your body or clothing. You may be attacked." "So potent, so powerful, no buck can resist!"—yet I was just as likely to generate a positive response (that is, attract a deer's attention) if I put down nothing or urinated on the site myself! These results would make one feel a bit foolish for paying money to apply one of their products—but as a group we are paying to the tune of millions of dollars a year.

Once again, I am not saying these products don't work (frankly, I have no idea whether they do). I am only saying they won't work as advertised over the vast majority of the whitetails' range because of the unnatural condition most of our herds are in.

The results I obtained while calling were far less clear.

I called on more than two hundred occasions, more than half the time to deer I could see, and I used all of the popular types of calls on the market. Never once did a call bring a deer in. A great many deer did react, though, with a kind of interest or hesitancy, and on several occasions, this hesitancy would have permitted me to get off shots I would not otherwise have risked. The problem was that, as far as I could tell, this sort of reaction only once involved a buck!

While archery hunting in October 1992, I heard clear sounds of running deer in a thicket in front of me. Then I heard a buck grunting behind where I'd heard the running deer. Figuring it was a buck trailing or running a doe, I waited to see what would happen. When the doe stepped out into an opening, she was walking broadside at about forty yards—much too far for a shot if the buck stayed right on her tail, which I was sure he'd do. So I began using a grunt call, mimicking the buck's grunting a few seconds before. The doe showed no reaction whatsoever, but continued walking slowly across the opening. I continued soft, intermittent grunts, hoping that might lure the buck closer, but it didn't work. He came to the opening, still on the doe's trail, cast a glance in my direction, then followed her.

On many other occasions, I had deer linger in the area long enough to work downwind of me, catch my scent, and leave. The general curiosity of deer often causes them to have an interest in something, but it does not often cause them to approach the thing that has caught their attention.

What's the bottom line about the techniques of antler rattling, luring, and calling? Are they a total waste of time? No, I don't think so; however, their effective use requires some extremely exacting conditions, and without those conditions, the techniques probably serve to scare more deer (especially wary bucks) than they attract. With so many hunters afield trying these tactics, I believe the deer are being sensitized to avoid such noises and odors. If a hunter goes out, rattles a couple of times and leaves after several hours, and a deer that heard the sound comes through, picking up the hunter's smell, what message do you think the deer gets? I know what I'd think if I were a deer: Avoid that sound! Or, in the case of lures: Avoid that odor!

For the past few years I've been hunting around the Crystal Falls, Iron River area in the U.P. In the fall of 1993 I noticed something about the vast majority of harvested bucks I saw: all their tines were broken. None of these deer was "big," but a great many were respectable sixes and eights. They ranged from yearlings to two-and-one-half year-olds. Obviously, these young bucks, teen-agers, so to speak, had been very busy earlier that fall, determining their dominance rankings. Why? Because the scarcity of older bucks promoted these younger bucks into positions of more active breeding than they would have enjoyed in a more balanced herd.

For the techniques under consideration to be effective, their use should be limited to one of the following situations: (1) a significant number of bucks within the same age class or classes; (2) regions, or pockets, where the buck:doe ratio is more balanced than usual; (3) minimal hunting pressure, not only at the time, but for the previous year or more; and (4) a proper time frame—during the late prerut or during the very early stages of the rut itself.

The problem with such criteria as I've just outlined is that most often, especially in an unfamiliar area, the needed information is obtained in retrospect. Scouting is the only way to know beforehand.

In addition to the above criteria, my research shows that for rattling, luring, and calling to be effective, they should be employed only in heavy cover that shows obvious signs of current deer usage and (especially for lures) only in close proximity (five to ten yards) of well-used runways.

I have not described in detail the techniques of rattling, calling, and luring because there are excellent sources for this that are readily available. Following is a list of those I find to be the best.

BOOKS

Morris, David. *Hunting Trophy Whitetails.* Big Fork,
Montana: Venture Press, 1992.
I recommend the entire book for anyone interested in trophy hunting, but brief sections describe the techniques at hand:
Rattling: Chapter 19, p. 366, paragraph 2, starting with "Why," and pp. 368–378.
Calling: p. 387, paragraph 3 to the end of the section.
Scents: p. 392, all of paragraph 4.
Cartier, John O. *How to Get Your Deer.* Outdoor Life Books,
1986.
Rattling: Chapter 9, "The Truth About Rattling," is all very interesting, but I particularly like the section on p. 128, paragraph 7 to the end of the chapter (pay particular attention to the safety advice given!).
Wootter, John. *Hunting Trophy Deer.* New York: Winchester
Press, 1977.
Rattling: A good, concise description in Chapter 13, particularly pp. 147–154

VIDEOS

Fatal Calling. Quest Production Group.
This is an excellent video on the techniques of calling during all periods.

Whitetail Scent Secrets. Bob McGuire Productions.

This video does a good job of showing what are believed to be the basic uses of scent.

I want to warn you about the emphatic rhetoric expressed in these videos. Remember, these people each have something to sell. Our understanding of these techniques is so rudimentary that it would be a mistake to depend on the accuracy of any of this information. As research biologists learn more about the world of whitetail communication, today's knowledge will someday, no doubt, seem very naive. The information in the videos is just the best we have to work with at present.

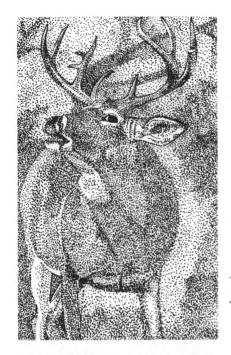

20

Miscellaneous Observations

There is a wealth of important information about deer behavior I observed while researching this book that wouldn't really fit into any of the previous chapters and that seems important enough to stand alone or bear repeating. Some of these observations were the result of questions I'd formulated before the field study, some were incidental observations that I had not anticipated—unexpected dividends, if you will. These topics are wideranging, but I hope you'll find the insights provided sufficiently enlightening to justify their inclusion.

DEER DISTRIBUTION PATTERNS

Within the area of my study lies a block of state land, roughly two square miles in size. It is very heavily used year-round. There's a large lake with a beach, boat rental, and picnic and camping areas. There are trails for hiking, cross-country skiing, and snowmobiling. In addition to the main entrance and parking areas, there are several smaller parking areas around the perimeter of the park, which are heavily used as entrance sites.

With the exception of 450-foot "safety zones" near the camping area, beach, and assorted buildings, the park land is open to hunting. It is very heavily hunted from mid-September until late January. I'd estimate that there's at least four or five times more hunting pressure on the park land than on the surrounding private lands that are used for hunting, and, of course, the state land is many, many times more heavily used for hiking, biking, skiing, and so forth.

In addition, nearly adjacent to the state land there is a two-section area of private land where there is no hunting at all. This land is used mostly by school and church groups for recreational hiking and camping. It sees heavy usage all summer, then weekend use from September through October, and again in late spring.

Most of the other land I researched experiences light to moderately heavy hunting pressure, with little intrusion otherwise (except for the farmland's farming-related activity). Taken as a whole, the lands in my study vary from good to excellent deer habitat.

Are there significant differences in the way the deer use these various types of land? Do the deer avoid the most heavily hunted (state) land and concentrate in the areas where hunting is banned? Does usage or avoidance of the land show consistent patterns according to the time of the year?

Before my study, I believed the deer would avoid the state land, especially during hunting seasons, and that they might mass up to some extent on the land that was closed to hunting and guns. What I found, however, was something quite different. On most occasions throughout the year (even during hunting seasons), I saw essentially the same distribution patterns among the deer. They were not evenly distributed over the land, but distribution did not seem to be determined in any way by hunting pressure. Instead, the deer distributed themselves according to the habitats they preferred at that particular season and according to their biological imperatives for that period, birthing or rutting needs, for example. Only after these needs were met did other factors, like hunting pressure or human intrusion, have some impact.

Factors other than human disturbance consistently proved to determine land choice by the deer. For example, the land used by church and school groups (closed to hunting) had very high deer numbers all winter in 1991, compared with the surrounding lands, but it was not the absence of hunters that caused this; it was because this area is heavily covered with mast-bearing oaks—more so than any other area in my study—and the autumn of 1990 had a record mast crop. The mast was so heavy that despite the deer feeding on it all autumn, the mast was still plentiful all winter, so the deer stayed there to feed on it. That winter, wherever there were stands of oaks, the deer were concentrated—even on the state land. In 1992 and especially in 1993, when the mast crop failed entirely, few deer could be found in the hardwoods anywhere, including the nonhunted lands. In some hardwoods that year I saw no deer at all.

In short, whatever patterns I found among the deer in one place, I found among the deer everywhere. For example, in early spring, when the deer are in their hyperactive mode (roughly end of March till end of April), they're in that mode everywhere, including the state land. They utilize the same types of cover, bed in comparable places, and feed on similar food types regardless of what kind of land they're on.

If deer activity and behaviors are the same regardless of land use, does that mean there's no difference based on the level or intensity of disturbance? No! I found there are some consistent differences in deer density as a result of human intrusion. The state land had far fewer deer than surrounding areas—about one-fifth as many—at all times of year.

Before my study, I predicted the deer would vacate the state land when hunting season arrived. I didn't think the does would drop their fawns there, either, but they did. I was surprised to find that no matter how intense the hunting pressure—and I would call it intense when on opening day and weekends there can be a deer hunter for every ten acres—some deer stay on the state land. It would be very interesting to know if the ones that stay are a small percentage of the deer that live in the area or if they are different deer whose normal range happens to include the state land and so they continue to use it intermittently despite the hunting pressure.

I also believed, prior to my study, that the deer would probably mass up, at least to some extent, in those areas closed to hunting, but I saw absolutely no indication of this. Several studies had shown what I later found myself, but I had doubted their validity, especially with pressure as intense as it is in my area.

What I found, as I have described in earlier chapters, is that deer respond to hunting pressure by becoming nocturnal, bedding in dense escape cover, and feeding within cover. They respond to very high levels of year-round human disturbance by avoiding the areas affected (though

With only one fairly consistent exception, big mature bucks always orientate themselves to protective cover. When "pressure" becomes more intense, this habit is only intensified. The exception? The "chase" phase of the rut—that two- to three-week period of exceptionally high buck activity prior to the actual "breeding" phase of the rut.

not abandoning them entirely), by staying in thicker cover a higher percentage of time, and perhaps by being even more nocturnal than deer in less-pressured areas.

Is there consistency in how deer utilize crop fields? Other feeding sites? Cover?

To answer these questions, I repeatedly estimated usage evident in fields, woodlots, swamps, brush, and so forth, and made pellet counts in these areas. Here's what I found.

CROP FIELDS

Two patterns are very clear. First, where fields are in such an area that the deer are exposed to possible disturbances, e.g., road traffic, the deer invariably use those portions of the field farthest from the source of possible interference. Second, no matter what crop is planted, if the field is good size (five acres or more), the great majority of its usage will be along the edges only.

If a field is both subject to disturbance and good size, then these tendencies are even more marked.

As poaching pressure mounted (late September through late December), some fields that were particularly vulnerable were all but abandoned by the deer.

ESCAPE COVER AREAS

This area could be brush, swamp, planted pines, mixed woodlots, or thickets within more open woodlots. For much of the year these areas show more sign of activity along their borders than in their interiors, but when hunting/poaching pressure mounts, their interior usage increases greatly.

OPEN WOODLOTS

Daytime usage is much higher in those areas that are immediately adjacent to escape cover. This becomes even more evident when hunting pressure mounts in the fall. If that pressure is intense, these areas cease to have daytime use altogether.

Do pastured cattle affect the deer's usage of an area? I had an opportunity to study this matter when a neighbor with two hundred acres suddenly pastured about fifty head of cattle on his land and simply let them run loose. Since I'd already established base levels of deer activity for this area, I was already halfway toward an answer.

I found that the cattle definitely do have an impact on the deer. I'd read several reports that cattle do not affect deer usage of an area, but several landowners in my study area are dairy farmers, and I've noticed that although I often see some deer in their pastures, I see more deer in the surrounding areas that do not have cattle.

After the cattle were turned loose on his two hundred acres, my neighbor's deer herd decreased by almost half within two or three months, and deer sightings in the area immediately adjacent to where the cattle were at any given time decreased to one-tenth of their previous level! This finding is so dramatic as to establish with certainty that the cattle have an impact on the deer (while not driving them away entirely).

Perhaps the reason lies in feeding competition, with the cattle eating some of the deer's preferred foods; perhaps the deer feel intimidated by the presence of the cattle. Whatever the reason, if deer have a choice of moving into a comparable area not shared by the cattle, I believe they'll do so.

How do deer react to farmers working their fields? A few months into my study, I noticed a definite reaction from the deer when a local farmer began working his fields in the spring. When he tilled his first field he did so in the afternoon, working straight into evening. The next morning, I was trying to get to some cover beyond the field; walking the field's perimeter, I noticed lots of deer tracks entering and leaving the field. Remember, this was a barren field, freshly plowed, with nothing in it. Yet the deer had investigated it thoroughly in less than twelve hours. This piqued my curiosity. The next field my neighbor plowed, I was right there the following morning again. Same thing; the deer had immediately checked out this field, too. On the next fields, I discovered something even more remarkable. It took only two fields for the deer to realize that there was nothing there for them—and they stopped investigating. By the time my neighbor had plowed four or five fields, days would go by without my finding a single deer track, and when I did, they were no longer the wandering, ambling tracks of deer investigating something, but rather the straight-line tracks of deer moving from one place to another across barren space.

Interestingly, the same investigatory behavior reappeared the next spring when the farmer plowed the same fields. The deer had learned very quickly, but by the following spring, they had to learn all over again.

In the early autumn (September 21), I was taking my evening drive and noticed a farmer harvesting a soybean field in which I had often seen deer. My first thought was, "Well, I won't see any deer here tonight," but as I got closer I saw two deer—a doe and a fawn—feeding less than a hundred yards from the farmer! They completely ignored the farmer, as if they had decided he posed no threat.

I found this pattern repeatedly: when farmers harvest their fields, the deer respond immediately, as soon as the farmer leaves or as soon as dusk comes, and they continue to feed in those fields as long as any spilled grains remain or until deep snow makes it too hard to find the grains.

Do deer move differently through open areas from the way they move through cover? How do they move while feeding or looking for bedding sites?

If you're a hunter, you've probably read about the value of preseason scouting. But what should you look for, and what will it tell you? One of the most informative things you can discover is how deer move when going about their day-to-day activities. When deer move across openings, if they're not feeding, it's in a straight line. They don't wander about; they seem to know where they're going, and they go there directly. When they're feeding, however, they do wander from location to location, first one way, then another. Even if they head in essentially one direction, they move in a wandering line. If you see that kind of movement, you will probably be able to see what they are feeding on. This is important to know, because all deer in that general area will be feeding on essentially the same items at any given time.

Within cover, it's a bit more complicated. If deer are just passing through, it will again be in a straight-line movement, and it will usually be on runways. If the deer are going to bed in the cover, it will also be straight-line movement until they near their bedding site—unless they're feeding, too, in which case they'll start to wander or, even more often, to circle the site downwind and return. They may search for an elevated position from which they can watch their entrance point. If the deer are feeding in cover, they'll wander randomly, but most generally along the perimeter of the area because that is where food is most available.

MOVEMENT RELATIVE TO WIND

Is there consistency in the way deer move in relation to the wind? Do they move differently when disturbed than when undisturbed? When in cover than when in the open?

I was eager to investigate this because I've often read that deer like to feed and move into the wind. But if that were true, wouldn't all our deer end up on the West Coast? So I observed closely, keeping wind direction in mind. My conclusion is that wind has little bearing on normal deer movement, other than the influences I discussed in Chapters 17 and 18. I find that deer move in the directions they do because of the cover available, the location of the food they want, and the lay of the land.

Out of a total of 1,298 deer that I observed in relation to the wind, 386 headed upwind (into the wind), 394 headed downwind (that is, with the wind), and 518 moved across the wind. Because there are two ways to move across the wind but only one way each to move into or with the wind, you'd expect a higher number to move crosswind (if wind has no bearing)—and that's exactly what I found.

I found it interesting that the times around hunting seasons (October, November, and December) showed no difference; percentages for these times were not significantly different from any other time of year. I had little chance to view deer under hunting pressure, so I can't comment on the effect of hunting pressure on their movements, but I can say that under all other conditions, they move uninfluenced by wind direction—at least in the Great Lakes region. The reason for that proviso is that in the Great Lakes region, our winds are fickle. We get a lot of swirling winds, as well as rapid and frequent changes in wind direction. Perhaps wind affects deer movement more noticeably in other regions; I cannot say.

In relation to the wind, I noted no differences among bucks, does, and fawns. Nor did I detect a difference in the way deer feed, in relation to the wind; they go wherever the food is.

FLAG RAISING

Are there times or circumstances that dictate or predict whether or not deer raise their flags? Are they more likely to do so in groups? Alone? At any particular time of year? In cover or in the open? Are bucks less likely to raise their flags than does?

Out of 1,060 deer observations in which I could tell whether they had raised their flags, 788 had them raised, 272 did not. I could determine no difference as to sex, type of cover, nor time of year. I only included observations where I was certain of gender and certain whether their tails were raised. Consequently, my numbers are low, and I'm not certain whether they are statistically reliable. Out of twenty bucks, twelve had tails up, eight kept them down. Of those that raised their tails, four were in open woods, four in thick cover, and four in open areas. Of the eight that didn't raise their tails, four were in heavy cover, two were in open woods, and two were in open areas.

I noticed a few curious things, for which I have no explanation whatsoever. Often I'd jump deer from the exact same location, leading to the assumption that they were, in fact, the same deer. One day they'd raise their flags, the next day they might not. On many occasions I noticed that some deer in a group would elevate their flags while other deer in the group would not. On the basis of my observations, about all I can say is that if you jump a southern Michigan deer, about two-thirds of the time it will raise its flag—regardless of sex, weather, type of cover, time of the year, or anything else—and about one-third of the time it won't.

VOCALIZATION

Are deer more likely to snort or "blow" when they can't smell you or when they can? Are they more likely to snort when in a group or when alone? More likely in the open or in cover? I wanted to answer these questions because I'm convinced that regional differences exist in how vocal deer are. I find, for example, that deer in northern Michigan are more vocal than those in southern Michigan, and I believe that whitetails in South Dakota's Black Hills are less vocal than those in northern Michigan.

The results of my observations do not prove these hypotheses, but they do show that southeastern Michigan deer are not very vocal. Of some eleven thousand deer I jumped and could determine one way or the other, only ninety-four (0.9 percent) snorted at me.

I do a lot of hunting, photographing, and observing of deer during the chase phase of the rut, when bucks are reported to be quite vocal—but I heard bucks grunting on only fourteen occasions in the past three years. This finding may be influenced by the fact that there are so few mature bucks in my study area. I don't know if mature deer are more vocal than younger deer. I've never read any opinion on whether vocalization is a function of age.

REACTIONS TO STIMULI

Is there a pattern in what deer react to and what they ignore? Throughout my observation of animals, what has fascinated me most is how they react to different stimuli.

My observations permit me to conclude that deer are exceedingly alert most of the time and that they're highly intelligent, able to distinguish immediately between innocuous and threatening sounds and events.

On countless occasions, I've been moving through an area very quietly, shielded from view, and downwind. Yet when I get to a spot where I see the deer, more often than not they've already been aware of my presence. I do sneak up on enough of them that I'm always hopeful of doing so, but it's a low percentage of the time.

Researchers claim that deer are vocal animals, and they've identified at least ten or twelve different vocal and nasal sounds that deer routinely make. It's important to realize, too, that all of these are short-range sounds, with the possible exception of the familiar "snort" (an alarm signal). It's unlikely that any of them can be heard at more than a hundred yards or so, even with the deers' keen auditory acuity. Buck "grunts," fawn "bleats," doe "mewing," and all lesser sounds, are hard for a human to hear at more than thirty or forty yards! In literally thousands of encounters I have annually with deer, it's far more common—all but 3 to 5 percent of the time—for deer to sneak or run off silently than to draw more attention to themselves through any form of vocalization.

For many years I've hunted and photographed in our western states. In that arid or semiarid environment, it is much easier to approach unsuspecting deer than in most other places. This is especially true of deer other than whitetails. I'm convinced that whitetails are the most alert animals in North America, if not in the world. If you can successfully stalk whitetails, you can stalk anything!

In late January 1991, I was out studying sign when I began hearing dogs barking. Within moments, a group of about twelve deer came racing through the woods, running away from the dogs. A couple of my neighbors were rabbit hunting, and the barking of their free-running dogs had immediately set the deer to flight; but the barking of those same dogs when they were tied up or kenneled was totally ignored by the deer. The deer also seem to know there is no threat from certain other neighborhood dogs that are untied but never (or rarely) leave their yards.

I have a neighbor who has one of those obnoxious dogs that barks all the time. When I've been out, I've heard that dog barking from far away; yet, more times than I can count, when I've gotten nearby, I've jumped deer. As long as the dogs are where the deer are accustomed to hearing them, they ignore them completely.

Traffic noise works the same way. No matter how noisy the vehicles are going down a roadway, the deer ignore them and feed or even bed within yards of the road. But if a vehicle leaves the road or goes down a seldom-used trail, the deer react immediately.

Following are lists of things I've seen deer ignore (or, at least, not react to visibly) and things I've seen deer react to:

Things Ignored

crows cawing
geese honking (even the first geese in spring)
blue jays squawking
ducks quacking
air raid/volunteer firemen siren
woodpeckers hammering
rooster pheasant crowing
raccoon running through the woods
two bucks sparring
horse in pasture (the horse also ignored the deer)
gun shots (even very nearby—see below)

Things Reacted to

hawk squealing in flight
sounds of animal running
sound of leaves rustling
rabbit running through the woods (deer looked in that
    direction, then resumed feeding)
deer decoy (both "buck" and "doe" decoys)

Before I put an item in the above columns, I needed to know what the noise or disturbance was, and I needed to have a clear vision of the deer so I could determine whether the deer reacted. This was not always easy to do, and this is why there are so few items in the columns. Sometimes the deer paid attention by stopping an activity (feeding, say), showing a momentary alertness, and throwing a glance in that direction before resuming the activity.

I only added an item to a column after observing the deer behave identically on several occasions. Some items were slightly inconsistent. For example, most of the time the deer ignored blue jays squawking, but not every single time. Bucks sparring would be another example of a usual-but-not-always reaction.

Deer reaction to gunfire is a curious thing. I shoot skeet at a large gun club. The club property is heavily hunted (including for deer) and is surrounded by state land. The surrounding deer population is low, probably about four or five per square mile, and the few deer present are extremely skittish and very alert. They don't make many mistakes when out in the hunting area; if they do, they die.

Former proprietors of the club used to feed the deer, and it was common for our shooting to be interrupted while the does, fawns, and bucks came in to feed. Many times, while shooters were standing on the pads shooting, the deer would come to station 8, where the owner had put out apples, carrots, grains, and the shooters had to wait because the deer would not leave!

Incidentally, feeding deer this way makes them so trusting they are pathetically vulnerable. One day when the club was closed, some low-life sneaked in and took advantage of the trusting deer; slaughtering several of them. It's too bad those of us who truly enjoy the deer have to worry about such scum, but we do.

Deer not accustomed to intense shooting, as these deer are, still show amazingly little reaction to it under most circumstances. A deer that is shot at or is with an animal that is shot will run pell-mell through cover for a short distance. But they'll only run far enough to be removed from the immediate area, then stop and assess their next move. I've seen this on many occasions. It's unusual for them to run more than two hundred yards, unless they're in the open (in which case, they'll run till they're in cover).

Many times I've seen deer feeding when gunfire erupts one or two hundred yards away. While they do cast inquiring glances or even stare intently in that direction, if nothing further happens, normally they'll continue their activity undisturbed.

Do deer hesitate to cross a creek or river when the place they routinely cross rises and becomes swollen—even if it is obvious that they could easily cross? Yes.

In the early spring of 1991, I was looking for sign and deer when I happened to jump a group of four. There were a couple inches of snow on the ground, so I began to track the deer. For several hundred yards they'd run straight down a runway. Off the hillside from which I'd jumped them, down into the bottoms they went, across a swollen, flooded area of standing water, to the banks of a nearby creek. There, they milled about, starting in one direction, then turning and paralleling the creek. Finally they turned away from the creek and ran back across the flooded flats, back up the hillside from which I'd jumped them. The runway they'd been following crossed the creek, and from previous experience, I knew that deer going down that run usually crossed, too. But these hadn't. Since the creek was swollen from snow melt and recent rain, I began to wonder if that was why the deer had turned back. I began checking the runs that crossed the creek, both that day and every time the creek was swollen for the next three years. I found an unmistakable pattern.

This particular creek is quite small; I can jump it in most places. It's steep-banked and normally the water in it—about six inches deep—is three feet lower than the surrounding ground, When swollen, it doesn't usually flood its banks, but sometimes it does. Many runways cross this creek in that particular area. Sometimes the deer walk across by going down one bank and up the other; just as often, they jump the creek.

The creek makes a lot more noise, of course, when it's swollen, and it flows much more swiftly. Under those circumstances, most of the time the deer will not cross it; they'll move just like the deer I tracked. This is one of those little tidbits of information that a hunter should tuck away; it could prove valuable some day.

BROWSING BEHAVIOR

Do deer browse more heavily on trees or large limbs that have blown over than they do on living upright trees? Surprisingly, yes. In the spring of 1991 we had a tornado move through my study area, uprooting a lot of trees. With maple and white pine trees in particular, I noticed something that seemed strange. Living, healthy, upright trees of these species are not normally browsed much by the deer in my study area, especially at that time of year. But the deer were browsing these toppled trees. I wondered why.

In late summer of 1991 we had a violent wind storm that toppled more trees, and again I noticed something odd. These trees had lain untouched for a couple weeks and then, seemingly overnight, the deer began to browse them heavily. I was at a complete loss to understand this behavior until I spoke with Glenn Dudderar from Michigan State University. Glenn is an associate professor in the Fisheries and Wildlife Department (and an extension specialist for the university), and he had a ready explanation.

"The best apples grow on the upper third of the tree. Because they get more sunlight, apples on those upper limbs have more nutrients—compared to the lower limbs, they're a powerhouse of nutrients, very rich in carbohydrates."

Why had the limbs lain untouched for a couple weeks before the deer ate them? "Simple. Those limbs were sepa-

Wind-toppled trees, limbs, and fruits can, and often will, quickly become a focal point for deer. This white pine limb was stripped bare, literally within hours of the time it had been blown out of the tree top.

rated from the tree, but they weren't done photosynthesizing. Because they still had their leaves, they continued to produce carbohydrates, but being now separated from the root system, the sugars couldn't be pumped away as they normally are. When they built up to a high concentration, they became particularly interesting for the deer to eat."

Simple for you, Glenn, not so simple for the rest of us. Thanks for solving the mystery.

DECOYS

In the past three or four years much has been written about deer decoys. The subject is definitely one of the "hot" topics in hunting circles these days, and many photographers talk about using them. Do they work as advertised? Do they really affect deer behavior? Do they really attract deer? Are they a useful tool for the archer (they are positively dangerous and should never be used by gun hunters) and photographer?

In an attempt to answer these questions I purchased a decoy (with detachable antlers, so I'd have both a buck and a doe decoy) in 1994. I used it through several months of photographic work and, believe me, it definitely had an impact on deer behavior! Not, however, in the way any hunter/photographer would desire. Put a decoy out and every single deer entering the area, where it can see the decoy, responds to it immediately. They'll stare, they'll stop, they'll often leave, they'll circle downwind. Very rarely would adult deer approach my decoy and, when they did, they were does only. I never once had a buck approach closer than thirty yards or so and even that was very rare. Most of the time, adult deer warily viewed the decoy from a long way off. Fawns did show less fear and heightened interest, and oftentimes they would approach the decoy. Interestingly, buck fawns were far more interested in the decoy than were doe fawns.

Because of the prevalence of poaching in my area, I stopped using the decoy around the middle of September, so I can't say for certain what deer would do later in the autumn period. Through all the months I did use the decoy, however, one thing was clearly more evident than anything else: Every deer, without exception, had a very dramatic reaction to the sight of the decoy. Their body language showed they were agitated, and suspicious. Now I'll simply ask you: Why, when we all go to great pains to avoid alarming the deer we seek to observe, hunt, or photograph, would we intentionally do anything to make them suspicious? Other than to study further the deer's reactions, I'll never use a deer decoy.

Knowledge is powerful; it makes all the difference. Its pursuit sustained me through three demanding years of observation and recording. Knowledge is the reward that makes the study of animals so fascinating and so gratifying!

Leonard Lee Rue once wrote a column wherein he spoke of buck fawns as being more daring, adventurous, inquisitive, and normally active than their female siblings. I got a kick out of it when a month or two later a female reader wrote to the magazine that it would be just as easy, and perhaps more descriptive, to call the young bucks' actions "stupid!" I don't pretend to know if buck fawns are more "daring" or more "stupid" than their sisters, but I can attest that behaviorally they're much different. The pair pictured here are a case in point. The buck (with his backside to the camera) was intensely interested in the decoy, while his sister (standing broadside to the camera) was content to feed and totally ignore it. For more than half an hour the buck ran around the decoy; he'd sneak up behind it, smell it, sometimes even touch it, only to race away and then approach it from a different angle. His sister finally got so bored with his antics that she wandered perhaps thirty feet away and lay down. It was only after I began to approach the decoy at dusk that the buck finally ran off.

Epilogue

I don't know how I came to be the hunter I am: I'm rigid and uncompromising in my beliefs about what hunting should be, and how it should be done. Somehow I grew up—long before I ever hunted—with the romantic notion of what a hunter should be. He's a lone individual, self-sufficient, who must be capable of going into the wilds, on foot, with little equipment—save that which will enable him to make quick, clean, and humane kills—and then leaving without a trace. He should be gentle, quiet, and respectful. He should know all he possibly can about the animals he hunts. He only takes what he needs, and he never attempts to take what he's after unless he's certain of his ability to make a clean kill. He does all he can to enhance his skills and abilities. He gladly accepts his responsibility to help wildlife and instill in others his vision.

The reality I've seen in more than forty years of hunting is somehow very different than my vision. I've always had an uneasiness about what I perceived to be the reality of hunting. Researching the material in this book helped crystallize that uneasiness. Hunting, as it's practiced today, does not even begin to approach my idealistic standards. Whether the ethical standards of today's hunters have slipped or never existed, I can't say for sure.

I had a really discouraging experience this past fall. I was invited to hunt a private ranch in southwest Texas. The couple who own the ranch are wonderful folks, very hospitable, friendly, and insightful. They made no bones about it, they are extremely reluctant to have hunters on their place. Nellieanna quite frankly admitted that essentially she's an antihunter; George is a former hunter, but no longer does so, in large measure because of how he witnessed other hunters behaving when he was afield. They had the insight, however, to hire a wildlife biologist to help them manage their land properly—to optimize its potential for *all* their wildlife. The biologist came in, assessed the land's needs, discussed their vision with them, and offered a management plan. One of the key elements was, of course, to keep the deer population within the constraints of the habitat. Like it or not, controlled hunting was going to be an integral part of their management plan! I was fortunate enough to be invited to hunt. The hunt itself was an incredible experience. I've never in my life seen as many "big" bucks as I saw there, and I've never seen a more balanced deer herd. I easily saw one buck for every doe and fawn I saw. That's what a deer herd should be!

What then was so discouraging? I spent eight days on the ranch, and when I wasn't hunting or photographing I was talking to George and Nellieanna. We got to know each other very well. We talked a lot about hunting and ethics. They got to hear my vision, and I heard theirs. Finally, near the end of my time there, they asked if I could recommend anyone to come and hunt with them. I couldn't! I've hunted, fished and been around shooters essentially all my life, and I couldn't think of anyone that had the sort of philosophical and ethical standards these folks wanted in their hunters! It's not that their standards are that high. It's not too much that landowners want their hunters to be skilled, respectful, thoughtful, courteous, and knowledgeable is it? And yet I couldn't, in good conscience, recommend anyone. After I returned from that trip I did think of a couple gentlemen who I have since recommended, but that truly is a sad commentary on the state of today's hunters. Like it or not, any hunters reading this, it is how I feel; much more germane, from my experiences talking to untold numbers of non-hunters, it's how the great majority of them feel too. It bothers me tremendously when I read that it's "a small minority" of hunters giving the activity a bad name today; from my experiences, it's not a small minority but a large percentage!

I do know that I'll never lower my standards. Don't misunderstand me; I've done some things in my hunting career I wish I could undo. I'm an avid waterfowl hunter, and in my younger days, on many occasions, I took much more than my legal limits. One deer season, I took two whitetails when I was only entitled to one. Things like this are not justifiable, they're the product of reckless insensitivity. But, I've been lucky. Through the years, it's been my good fortune to have met some wonderful sportsmen (and women), who had the standards I now share. I truly admired and respected these people; I have emulated, and in many cases expanded, their example. I learned, and I grew. Unfortunately, all the truly wonderful sportsmen I've known, like the three this book is dedicated to, are now gone.

I have no right to tell others how to hunt. I have no right to impose my will, my thoughts, my beliefs, on them. But the electorate of this country do, and I believe that unless the hunting fraternity begins to accept its responsibility for the elevation of ethical standards, we *will* lose our hunting privileges. I truly believe that, and I don't think that day is far off.

In 1994, Jim Posewitz, a wildlife biologist for thirty-two years with the Montana Department of Fish, Wildlife & Parks, wrote a book titled *Beyond Fair Chase: The Ethic and Tradition of Hunting*. For anyone who has the slightest interest in this whole issue, I strongly recommend them to read this wonderful little book. If hunting is to survive (and I fervently believe that for the welfare of our wildlife, it must), the ideas expressed in Jim's book *must be adopted*, even expanded, by all hunters.

Beyond Fair Chase can be purchased from:
Falcon Press Publishing Co., Inc.
P.O. Box 1718
Helena, Montana 59624

Let's use all our wisdom and knowledge to ensure the continual presence and vitality of such a magnificent creature as the white-tailed deer. They deserve nothing less than the best we can do for them—ensure their healthy future, forever.

Glossary

aggregate group(s). Deer for most of the year are segregated into two types of groups: maternal family units, and bachelor groups. When, because of diminished resources, deer come together into larger nonrelated, mixed groups, these groups are known as aggregate groups.

bachelor group(s). A grouping of deer consisting of bucks only. Size varies, normally from as few as two to as many as seven or eight, perhaps even more in well-balanced deer herds.

blastocyst. The developing ovum, after a spherical cavity has formed, but prior to implantation. Although cellular cleavage has occurred prior to this embryonic stage, cellular differentiation has not.

blastoderm. The developmental stage following the blastocyst form, when cellular specialization has occurred. All three primary layers are present: the ectoderm, mesoderm, and entoderm.

browsers. Animals that feed primarily, or completely, on woody growth tissues or their offshoots, such as tree leaves. As opposed to "grazers," animals that primarily feed on nonwoody vegetation, such as grasses and forbs. In reality most (but not all) herbivores are a combination of both. The whitetail certainly is.

buck sign. Refers collectively to the physical, visual, and olfactory evidence that male deer leave as to their presence and identity. Generally indicates the scrapes and rubs that bucks create during the various phases of the rutting period.

catabolism. The physiological process of breaking down nutrients within the body of an organism. Metabolism has two components: catabolism, the breaking down of complex molecules and chemicals into more usable forms, and anabolism, the building up of complex chemicals from simpler ones. Catabolism produces energy, anabolism requires energy input.

calls. Sounds produced in order to attract an animal. Also refers to the vehicle with which those sounds are produced. Some such vehicles are manufactured, some are purely vocal. Native Americans (and natives in other areas of the world) were experts at mimicking animal sounds, usually vocally. The art is still practiced today by some hunters and naturalists.

carrying capacity. The ability of a particular area to support the animals present, without sustaining decreased capacity in the future. Also, the number of animals thus supported. This ability fluctuates all the time, and for the well-being of both the animals and the habitat, it must be kept in balance.

cohort. A collection of animals of the same sex and species that are all the same age.

compensatory mortality. A phenomenon whereby one cause of mortality replaces another. For example, hunters culling animals prevents the winter starvation and the spread of diseases from which those animals would die had the hunters not taken them first. Diseases spread more rapidly, and starvation is more widespread in herds with higher densities, therefore the mortality from hunting is oftentimes compensatory.

conterminous. Two or more species of animals that occupy the same range.

crepuscular. Customarily active in dim light, i.e., early and late in the day (twilight), as is the whitetail.

dam. The mother of a deer. (Said of quadrupeds in general.)

duff. The assorted materials—leaves, twigs, decaying vegetation—that normally cover the ground.

embryo. The product of conception during its early stages of development, prior to becoming a fetus; usually the first trimester.

estrus. The period of ovulation or sexual receptiveness in female mammals other than humans. (Also called "heat.")

fetus. That stage in prenatal development following complete organ differentiation, usually comprising the second and third trimesters.

Flehmen. The behavior a rutting buck demonstrates after tasting doe urine. Also called "lip curling." Named after the man who first described the behavior.

grazers. Herbivores who habitually, or routinely, feed on grasses and forbs as opposed to woody vegetation or its offshoots (see **browsers**).

herbivores. Animals that eat plants. As opposed to carnivores, (meat eaters) or omnivores (eaters of both plants and meat). Although whitetails are considered by all to be herbivores, they have on occasion been known to eat meat. It's believed that on those occasions when they do so they are attempting to extract certain minerals from the food that they are deficient in at that time. Has to be considered rare.

home range or territory. The area in which a particular whitetail normally lives. It is not defended, except in the case of does with newborn fawns (less than one month old).

implantation. The process a fertilized ovum undergoes in becoming attached to the uterine wall, so that maternal nourishing can begin. Prior to implantation all nutrients are derived from the yolk of the egg.

innate. Instinctual, as opposed to learned, behaviors in an animal.

juvenile. In the case of white-tailed deer, an animal between five or six months (recruitment age) and one year of age.

learned. Behaviors that are acquired through time, observation, and experience, as opposed to innate.

lip curl. (See **Flehmen**.)

lipogenesis. The formation and accumulation of fat depots in various sites throughout the body. Most generally in the whitetail it refers to abdominal and bone marrow deposits. This is an obligatory process that occurs in the late summer/autumn period each year.

maternal family unit. All the blood-related deer that a female whitetail habitually associates with. This group includes their young male offspring (less than one year of age).

metabolic rate. The rate at which the body of any organism burns energy. There are different rates depending on what the organism is doing. The rate at rest is called the basal metabolic rate (BMR); the rate increases, of course, with activity, and the time of year.

monoculture. Refers to a single-species form of growth, be it trees, crops, or other life forms.

monophagus. An animal that normally consumes only one food source.

morphological. Pertaining to the form and structure of living organisms or parts thereof.

multipara. A (pregnant) female that has given birth previously.

olfactory. Pertaining to the sense of smell.

ovum. The female reproductive cell.

parasite. An organism that feeds off of another organism and contributes nothing to the survival of its host. As opposed to a symbiont, or a symbiotic relationship, where there is some mutual benefit.

parasite load. The total number of parasites that an animal has at any given time.

pedicles. The base upon which a buck's antlers grow. It's actually a specialized section of the frontal bone in the deer's skull. There's one for each antler.

physical dimorphism. The differential development that some twins undergo whereby they develop at different rates.

primipara. A (pregnant) female that has not given birth previously.

recruitment. Refers to that collection of fawns that survive at least to their first autumn. It's used because the survivability of newborn fawns is so difficult to assess accurately, and is so variable.

refreshen (also **rework**). The process a deer (may be a buck, doe, or fawn) goes through in redoing an existing rub, scrape, or licking branch.

riparian. Pertaining to the banks and flood plain of a creek, river, pond or lake.

riverine. Same as **riparian** above.

rub. Usually a damaged area of a tree or bush, but can be a fencepost or even a telephone pole, caused by a buck rubbing his polished antlers against it.

rub-urination. The act of a deer (usually, but not always, a buck) urinating so that the urine dribbles down his legs and across his tarsal glands as he then rubs them together, thereby mixing the urine and his glandular secretions together. Normally done over, and thus deposited on, a scrape site.

rut. The period of time when deer of both sexes undergo the physiological, psychological, and behavioral requisites to ensure successful breeding. Includes the "prerut" phase, the actual "breeding" phase, and the "postrut" phase. Each of these phases of the rut can be further subdivided for very technical discussions of breeding-related behaviors and changes.

scent. An odor left by an animal, or made to imitate an animal's odor. May be natural or artificial.

scrape. An area where a buck or doe has pawed clear the litter and duff normally present, thus exposing the soil and leaving an individual odor in order to be identified as the maker of the scrape. Normally shows a footprint (sometimes more than one), smells of urine, may have fecal pellets on it, and usually has an associated overhanging tree branch upon which the deer has also deposited scent. They are thought to be critical to the timing and synchronization of rutting activity.

senescence. The process of aging or growing old.

sign. Visible and olfactory evidence animals leave of their presence. In the case of deer it normally refers to tracks, droppings, rubs, scrapes, and licking branches.

sign making. The physical acts by which sign is made. Usually, but certainly not always, by bucks.

spar (**sparring**). What two or more bucks are said to do when they have polished antlers and use them to shove and push one another. This is thought to be a safe way for bucks in physical contact with one another to settle the issue of dominance prior to the actual time of breeding activity. It's an activity only seen during the prerut phase.

stereotypical. Innate behaviors by which animals instinctively know what's being communicated by others of their species. All members of that species and sex employ the same means of communication (often stereotypical behaviors are sexually dimorphic; that is, they assume separate forms between the sexes).

tending. What a buck does when he accompanies an estrous doe. A period of twenty-four to thirty-six hours.

territorial. When an animal defends a particular area in order to keep others of its species out of the area. The only time whitetails are territorial is when does defend a territory during, and immediately following, the birth of fawns.

velvet. A skinlike covering that begins growing on the surface of the pedicles at the beginning of the antler-growing cycle. Unless damaged it expands as the antlers grow, always covering them completely. It is the matrix in which the blood vessels supplying nutrients to the growing antlers are embedded.

vomeronasal. An organ system, common to "hoofed" mammals, thought to closely parallel and yet be totally independent of the olfactory system. It's believed to be more sensitive to molecules in solution (as opposed to volatile odors), such as estrous odors in urine, than is the olfactory system.

yearling. Technically, a deer that is between one and two years of age. However, often used to describe animals of ten or eleven months as well. Generally not used after the animal's second autumn.

yolk. The energy source within an ovum. Consists primarily of fats and protein.

Bibliography

Chapter 1

Forbes, S. E., L. M. Lang, S. A. Liscinsky, and H. A. Roberts. 1979. The white-tailed deer in Pennsylvania. *Res. Bull. 170.* Harrisburg: Pennsylvania Game Commission.

Hornacker, M. G. 1970. An analysis of mountain lion predation upon mule deer and elk in the Idaho primitive area. *Wildl. Monogr. 21.* Washington, D.C.: The Wildlife Society.

Knowlton, F. F. 1964. Aspects of coyote predation in south Texas with special reference to white-tailed deer. Ph.D. diss. Purdue.

Mech, L. D. 1970. *The wolf; the ecology and behavior of an endangered species.* Garden City, N.Y.: Natural History Press.

————. 1977a. Productivity, mortality and population trend in wolves form northeastern Minnesota. *J. Mammal.* 58 (4): 559–574.

———. 1977b. Wolf pack buffer zones as prey reservoirs. *Science* 198: 320–321.

Nelson, M. E., and L. D. Mech. 1981. Deer social organization and wolf predation in northeastern Minnesota. *Wildl. Monogr. 77.* Washington, D. C.: The Wildlife Society.

Niebauer, T. J., and O. J. Rongstad. 1977. Coyote food habits in northwestern Wisconsin. In *Proc. 1975 Predator Symp.*, ed. R. L. Phillips and C. Jonkel, 237–251, Montana For. Conserv. Exp. Stn. Missoula: University of Montana.

Ozoga, J. J., and E. M. Harger. 1966. Winter activities and feeding habits of northern Michigan coyotes. J. *Wildl. Manage.* 30 (4): 809–818.

Segelquist, C. A., F. D. Ward, and R. G. Leonard. 1969. Habitat-deer relations in two Ozark enclosures. *J. Wildl. Manage.* 33 (3): 511–520.

Chapter 2

Geist, Valerius. 1986. New evidence of high frequency of antler wounding in Cervids. *Canadian Journal of Zoology.* 64: 380–384.

Chapter 3

Lambiase, J. T., Jr., R. P. Amann, and J. S. Lindzey. 1972. Aspects of reproductive physiology of male white-tailed deer. *J. Wildl. Manage.* 36 (3): 868–875.

Woods, G. R. November 1993. *Deer & Deer Hunting Magazine.*

Chapter 6

Halls, Lowell K., ed. 1984. *White-tailed deer: Ecology and management*. A Wildlife Management Institute Book. Stackpole Books.

Robinette, W. L., J. S. Gashwiler, D. A. Jones, and H. S. Crane. 1955. Fertility of mule deer in Utah. *J. Wildl. manage*. 19 (1): 115–136.

Silver, H. 1961. Deer milk compared with substitute milk for fawns. *J. Wildl. Manage*. 25 (1): 66–70.

Verme, L. J. 1963. Effect of nutrition on growth of white-tailed deer fawns. *Trans. N. Amer. Wildl. and Natur. Resur. Conf*. 28: 431–443.

Chapter 8

Forbes, S. E., L. M. Lang, S. A. Liscinsky, and H. A. Roberts. 1979. The white-tailed deer in Pennsylvania. *Res. Bull. 170*. Harrisburg: Pennsylvania Game Commission.

Hornacker, M. G. 1970. An analysis of mountain lion predation upon mule deer and elk in the Idaho primitive area. *Wildl. Monogr. 21*. Washington, D. C.: The Wildlife Society.

Knowlton, F. F. 1964. Aspects of coyote predation in south Texas with special reference to white-tailed deer. Ph.D. diss. Purdue University,

Mech, L. D. 1970. *The wolf; the ecology and behavior of an endangered species*. Garden City, N.Y.: Natural History Press.

————. 1977a. Productivity, mortality and population trend in wolves form northeastern Minnesota. *J. Mammal*. 58 (4): 559–574.

————. 1977b. Wolf pack buffer zones as prey reservoirs. *Science* 198: 320–321.

Nelson, M. E., and L. D. Mech. 1981. Deer social organization and wolf predation in northeastern Minnesota. *Wildl. Monogr. 77.* Washington, D. C.: The Wildlife Society.

Niebauer, T. J., and O. J. Rongstad. 1977. Coyote food habits in northwestern Wisconsin. In *Proc. 1975 Predator Symp.*, ed. R. L. Phillips and C. Jonkel, 237–251, Montana For. Conserv. Exp. Stn. Missoula: University of Montana.

Ozoga, J. J., and E. M. Harger. 1966. Winter activities and feeding habits of northern Michigan coyotes. *J. Wildl. Manage.* 30 (4): 809–818.

Segelquist, C. A., F. D. Ward, and R. G. Leonard. 1969. Habitat-deer relations in two Ozark enclosures. *J. Wildl. Manage.* 33 (3): 511–520.

Chapter 9

Halls, Lowell K., ed. 1984. *White-tailed deer: Ecology and management.* A Wildlife Management Institute Book. Harrisburg, PA. Stackpole Books. 572.

Chapter 13

Woods, G. R. November 1993. January 1994. *Deer & Deer Hunting Magazine.*

Chapter 15

Atkeson, T. D., and R. L. Marchinton. 1982a. Scent communication in white-tail deer. Abstract. from Southeast Deer Study Group, 58–59.

Atkeson, T. D., and R. L. Marchinton. 1982b. Forehead glands in white-tailed deer. *J. Mammal.* 63 (4): 613–617.

Kile, K. L., and R. L. Marchinton. 1977. White-tailed deer rubs and scrapes: spatial, temporal, and physical characteristics and social role. *Amer. Midl. Natur.* 97 (2): 257–266.

Litchfield, T. R. 1987. Relationships among white-tailed deer rubbing, scraping, and breeding activities. Master's thesis, University of Georgia, 1987.

Marchinton, R. L., K. V. Miller, K. E. Kammermeyer, and E. B. Moser. 1987. Population and habitat influences on antler rubbing by white-tailed deer. *J. Wildl. Manage.* 51: 62–66.

Ozoga, J. J., and L. J. Verme. 1985. Comparative breeding behavior and performance of yearling vs. prime-age white-tailed bucks. *J. Wildl. Manage.* 49: 364–372.

Chapter 18

Marchinton, R. L., and L. K. Jeter. 1967. Telemetric study of deer movement-ecology in the Southeast. In *Proc. Ann. Conf. Southeast Assoc. Game and Fish Comm.* 20: 189–206.

Index